The Magic of
SPIN

AUSTRALIA'S
GREATEST
SPIN BOWLERS

Also by Ashley Mallett

Autobiography
Rowdy
Spin Out

Biography
Trumper: The Illustrated Biography
Clarrie Grimmett: The Bradman of Spin
Chappelli Speaks Out
One of a Kind: The Doug Walters Story
Nugget – Man of the Century
Scarlet: Clarrie Grimmett – Test cricketer
Thommo Speaks Out
No Beating About the Bush
The Diggers' Doctor

Historical
The Black Lords of Summer
The Catch that Broke a Bank
Great Australian Test Cricket Stories

General non-fiction
One Hundred Cricket Tips
In Bradman's Band
Eleven: The Greatest Eleven of the 20th Century
The Boys from St Francis

Children's
Master cricketer series: Allan Border; The Chappell Brothers;
Dennis Lillee; Don Bradman; Doug Walters; Geoff Lawson;
Kim Hughes; Rodney Marsh
Master footballer series: Mark Williams; Tim Watson; Robert Flower;
Wayne Johnston
Master soccer player series: John Kosmina
Master tennis player series: Evonne Cawley

The Magic of
SPIN

AUSTRALIA'S
GREATEST
SPIN BOWLERS

ASHLEY MALLETT

Hardie Grant

BOOKS

Published in 2019 by Hardie Grant Books,
an imprint of Hardie Grant Publishing

Hardie Grant Books (Melbourne)
Building 1, 658 Church Street
Richmond, Victoria 3121

Hardie Grant Books (London)
5th & 6th Floors
52–54 Southwark Street
London SE1 1UN

hardiegrantbooks.com

 A catalogue record for this
book is available from the
National Library of Australia

The Magic of Spin
ISBN 978 1 74379 578 1

Cover design by Luke Causby/Blue Cork
Typeset in 13.5/16 pt Granjon by Post Pre-Press Group
Printed in Australia by Griffin Press, part of Ovato, an Accredited
ISO AS/NZS 14001 Environmental Management System printer

 The paper this book is printed on is certified against
the Forest Stewardship Council® Standards. Griffin
Press holds FSC chain of custody certification
SGS-COC-005088. FSC promotes environmentally
responsible, socially beneficial and economically viable
management of the world's forests.

This book is dedicated to my wife, Patsy Mary Mallett,
the love of my life.

CONTENTS

FOREWORD

by Ian Chappell

Ashley 'Rowdy' Mallett was a fine off-spinner – tall but with the ability to make the ball dip from a point above the batsman's eye line and then turn when it landed, Mallett was blessed with the big heart so necessary to become a successful tweaker at international level. If you want a clue as to how good Mallett was as a spinner, he reached 100 Test wickets bowling less balls than it took Shane Warne to achieve that landmark.

I was fortunate enough to captain Mallett both at state and Test level, and he was a valued teammate both on and off the field. Of the many positive traits that Mallett possessed as a spin bowler, there was one that stood out: the better the batsman, the better he bowled.

When Greg Chappell first moved to Queensland, he came in to face Mallett on an Adelaide Oval pitch that was receptive to spin. Quite uncharacteristically Chappell lofted a few shots to the boundary in the first over. Mallett's next four overs to Chappell all resulted in maidens from hard-spun off-breaks that tested all the batsman's faculties.

After play I was having a beer with Chappell and I asked, 'You didn't think I was going to do something stupid out there, did you?'

'I was hoping,' he responded.

When I asked him how good those next four overs were, he just rolled his eyes and replied, 'As good as I've faced.'

Since retiring Mallett has been a prolific writer, employing his knowledge of the game and the characters who played it and spicing his work with his quirky sense of humour.

His humour, along with his renowned clumsiness, were endearing traits that made him an entertaining teammate. Whether he was doing a limp fall in the middle of a crowded room or spinning yarns about his 'employment' – ranging from film producer to stockbroker – at the interminable cocktail parties in the UK, there was never a dull moment when Mallett was about. To add colour to his yarns about his various 'jobs', he employed a full range of English accents from 'plum in the mouth posh' to 'within the sound of Bow Bells Cockney' with great effect.

Consequently, it's always been a pleasure to read Mallett's writing on spinners, and I've particularly enjoyed his insights on the ever-active mind of Clarrie 'The Fox' Grimmett and the ferociously competitive attitude of his bowling partner Bill 'Tiger' O'Reilly.

I experienced firsthand his dedication to writing when he published a well-researched book on me that I thought admirably captured my personality.

Having enjoyed many years playing and touring alongside Mallett, I'm now pleased to read his observations on the difficult art of spin bowling. No one is better qualified to write about the magic of spin through the decades than Ashley Mallett.

Mr Barry Jevon Smith
NHS Number: 4640386249
DoB: 13/04/1935
2 Larch End
West Chiltington
Pulborough
W Sussex
RH20 2QE

Pulborough Medical Group
Pulborough Primary Care
Centre Spiro Close
Pulborough
West Sussex
RH20 1FG

Prescription Start Date: 31/05/2023
Prescription Expiry Date: 30/11/2023

Patient Medication History
[ ] Atenolol 25mg tablets, 28 tablet, take one daily,
Last Issued: Wednesday 31 May 2023, Next Issue Due: Wed
28 Jun 2023, Review Due On: Fri 26 Jan 2024
[ ] Bendroflumethiazide 2.5mg tablets, 28 tablet, take
one each morning, Last Issued: Wednesday 31 May 2023,
Next Issue Due: Wed 28 Jun 2023, Review Due On: Fri 26
Jan 2024
[ ] Clopidogrel 75mg tablets, 28 tablet, take one once
daily, Additional Script Notes: Switched from Aspirin
to Clopidogrel by Vascular Surgeon, Last Issued:
Wednesday 31 May 2023, Next Issue Due: Wed 28 Jun 2023,
Review Due On: Fri 26 Jan 2024
[ ] Felodipine 5mg modified-release tablets, 28 tablet,
take one daily, Last Issued: Wednesday 31 May 2023,
Next Issue Due: Wed 28 Jun 2023, Review Due On: Fri 26
Jan 2024
[ ] Olmesartan medoxomil 10mg tablets, 28 tablet, take
one daily, Last Issued: Wednesday 31 May 2023, Next
Issue Due: Wed 28 Jun 2023, Review Due On: Fri 26 Jan
2024
[ ] Olmesartan medoxomil 20mg tablets, 28 tablet, take
one daily, Last Issued: Wednesday 31 May 2023, Next
Issue Due: Wed 28 Jun 2023, Review Due On: Fri 26 Jan
2024
[ ] Omeprazole 20mg gastro-resistant capsules, 28
capsule, take one daily so long as taking Clopidogrel,
Additional Script Notes: January 2019: patient has
stopped ordering this since September. Please check he
gets the one off message about Clopidogrel and the risk
of GI bleeds., Last Issued: Wednesday 31 May 2023, Next
Issue Due: Wed 28 Jun 2023, Review Due On: Fri 26 Jan

When should I pay?

You must pay if none of the statements apply to you on the day you were asked to pay. These are the only accepted reasons for not paying.

I'm not sure if I should pay

Pay and ask for a **prescription refund form (FP57)**. You can't get one later. If you find you didn't need to pay, you can claim a refund up to 3 months later.

What if I don't pay when I should?

We check claims made for free prescriptions. If we can't confirm that you are entitled to exemption from prescription charges, you may be issued a Penalty Charge Notice and you may have to pay up to £100 as well as your prescription charge(s), and you could be prosecuted.

Can I get help to pay?

Help with costs may be available. You could also save money by buying a prescription prepayment certificate.

Check at **www.nhsbsa.nhs.uk/check**

Is my exemption certificate still valid?

Visit www.nhsbsa.nhs.uk/exemption to see what help is available or ask at your GP surgery or pharmacy.

I am unable to collect my prescription

If you are unable to collect your prescription someone can do so on your behalf. Your representative should complete the 'If you paid' box and sign the form, or you or your representative should complete the 'If you didn't pay' box, and your representative should sign the form. Your representative will need to put a cross in the 'on behalf of patient' box next to their signature.

Why did the pharmacy ask to see evidence?

We need to check your exemption is valid.

The NHS Business Services Authority is responsible for this service. We will use your information to check your exemption is valid, pay the dispenser and help plan and improve NHS services. Find out more at www.nhsbsa.nhs.uk/yourinformation

Mr Barry Jevon Smith
NHS Number: 4640386249
DoB: 13/04/1935
2 Larch End
West Chiltington
Pulborough
W Sussex
RH20 2QE

Pulborough Medical Group
Pulborough Primary Care
Centre Spiro Close
Pulborough
West Sussex
RH20 1FG

Prescription Start Date: 31/05/2023
Prescription Expiry Date: 30/11/2023

Patient Medication History
[ ] Atenolol 25mg tablets, 28 tablet, take one daily,
Last Issued: Wednesday 31 May 2023, Next Issue Due: Wed
28 Jun 2023, Review Due On: Fri 26 Jan 2024
[ ] Bendroflumethiazide 2.5mg tablets, 28 tablet, take
one each morning, Last Issued: Wednesday 31 May 2023,
Next Issue Due: Wed 28 Jun 2023, Review Due On: Fri 26
Jan 2024
[ ] Clopidogrel 75mg tablets, 28 tablet, take one once
daily, Additional Script Notes: Switched from Aspirin
to Clopidogrel by Vascular Surgeon, Last Issued:
Wednesday 31 May 2023, Next Issue Due: Wed 28 Jun 2023,
Review Due On: Fri 26 Jan 2024
[ ] Felodipine 5mg modified-release tablets, 28 tablet,
take one daily, Last Issued: Wednesday 31 May 2023,
Next Issue Due: Wed 28 Jun 2023, Review Due On: Fri 26
Jan 2024
[ ] Olmesartan medoxomil 10mg tablets, 28 tablet, take
one daily, Last Issued: Wednesday 31 May 2023, Next
Issue Due: Wed 28 Jun 2023, Review Due On: Fri 26 Jan
2024
[ ] Olmesartan medoxomil 20mg tablets, 28 tablet, take
one daily, Last Issued: Wednesday 31 May 2023, Next
Issue Due: Wed 28 Jun 2023, Review Due On: Fri 26 Jan
2024
[ ] Omeprazole 20mg gastro-resistant capsules, 28
capsule, take one daily so long as taking Clopidogrel,
Additional Script Notes: January 2019: patient has
stopped ordering this since September. Please check he
gets the one off message about Clopidogrel and the risk
of GI bleeds., Last Issued: Wednesday 31 May 2023, Next
Issue Due: Wed 28 Jun 2023, Review Due On: Fri 26 Jan

When should I pay?

You must pay if none of the statements apply to you on the day you were asked to pay. These are the only accepted reasons for not paying.

I'm not sure if I should pay

Pay and ask for a **prescription refund form (FP57).** You can't get one later. If you find you didn't need to pay, you can claim a refund up to 3 months later.

What if I don't pay when I should?

We check claims made for free prescriptions. If we can't confirm that you are entitled to exemption from prescription charges, you may be issued a Penalty Charge Notice and you may have to pay up to £100 as well as your prescription charge(s), and you could be prosecuted.

Can I get help to pay?

Help with costs may be available. You could also save money by buying a prescription prepayment certificate.

Check at **www.nhsbsa.nhs.uk/check**

Is my exemption certificate still valid?

Visit www.nhsbsa.nhs.uk/exemption to see what help is available or ask at your GP surgery or pharmacy.

I am unable to collect my prescription

If you are unable to collect your prescription someone can do so on your behalf. Your representative should complete the 'If you paid' box and sign the form, or you or your representative should complete the 'If you didn't pay' box, and your representative should sign the form. Your representative will need to put a cross in the 'on behalf of patient' box next to their signature.

Why did the pharmacy ask to see evidence?

We need to check your exemption is valid.

The NHS Business Services Authority is responsible for this service. We will use your information to check your exemption is valid, pay the dispenser and help plan and improve NHS services. Find out more at www.nhsbsa.nhs.uk/yourinformation

Mr Barry Jevon Smith
NHS Number: 4640386249
DoB: 13/04/1935
2 Larch End
West Chiltington
Pulborough
W Sussex
RH20 2QE

Pulborough Medical Group
Pulborough Primary Care
Centre Spiro Close
Pulborough
West Sussex
RH20 1FG

2024

Patient Instructions
*** Due to high demand during December, please can you
request your medication at least 7 days before
collection from the pharmacy ***

When should I pay?

You must pay if none of the statements apply to you on the day you were asked to pay. These are the only accepted reasons for not paying.

I'm not sure if I should pay

Pay and ask for a **prescription refund form (FP57)**. You can't get one later. If you find you didn't need to pay, you can claim a refund up to 3 months later.

What if I don't pay when I should?

We check claims made for free prescriptions. If we can't confirm that you are entitled to exemption from prescription charges, you may be issued a Penalty Charge Notice and you may have to pay up to £100 as well as your prescription charge(s), and you could be prosecuted.

Can I get help to pay?

Help with costs may be available. You could also save money by buying a prescription prepayment certificate.

Check at **www.nhsbsa.nhs.uk/check**

Is my exemption certificate still valid?

Visit www.nhsbsa.nhs.uk/exemption to see what help is available or ask at your GP surgery or pharmacy.

I am unable to collect my prescription

If you are unable to collect your prescription someone can do so on your behalf. Your representative should complete the 'If you paid' box and sign the form, or you or your representative should complete the 'If you didn't pay' box, and your representative should sign the form. Your representative will need to put a cross in the 'on behalf of patient' box next to their signature.

Why did the pharmacy ask to see evidence?

We need to check your exemption is valid.

The NHS Business Services Authority is responsible for this service. We will use your information to check your exemption is valid, pay the dispenser and help plan and improve NHS services. Find out more at www.nhsbsa.nhs.uk/yourinformation

The Magic of Spin

He spins the ball so hard that it sings and it hums
the batsman's bemused all fingers and thumbs
It arrives in a curve, like the flight of an arrow
The Magic of Spin brings the boy to the barrow

Lara's bat and his pad is now slightly astray
the ball finds the gap and he leaves in dismay.
Bowled through the gate by a ball we are told,
Warne's leg break a thing to behold.

Would Bradman have tamed the genius of turn?
O bring on the challenge, the memory does burn.
Warney releases a ball of great danger
and Bradman spars at the fizzing stranger.

The ball fairly buzzes, an ace and a trump.
It pitches leg perfect and hits the off stump!

© Ashley Mallett

INTRODUCTION

Richie Benaud, like his hero Keith Miller, epitomised the daring of cricket. Benaud was a cricketing hero to me and my mates growing up in Sydney in the early to mid 1950s. We slapped on Brylcreem as though it was going out of fashion as a tribute to our cricket hero, much the same as other youngsters of the time tried to develop a kiss curl á la Bill Haley.

From the time we got home from school my elder brother, Nick, and I would get stuck into a game of cricket in our Chatswood backyard in suburban Sydney. The inevitable backyard 'Tests' were a joy as we emulated our heroes. I never got to emulate Benaud, however, for he was in the Australian team and I was instructed by Nick that I had to be England. But whenever Nick was not at home and I was left to my own devices, I would try to bowl like Benaud. The only concession from Nick was to allow me to have Victor Trumper as one of the England openers. Nick kept score in an old exercise book: every ball, every run to the batsman and runs taken off each bowler.

One of our rules was that you had to bowl in the same style as the bowler at the crease, so when the England captain Len Hutton called Jim Laker to the crease, I bowled off spin. It was Laker who inspired me to take up the art a few years later, in 1956, when he took 19 of Australia's 20 wickets on a treacherous turner at Old Trafford. I never lost my fascination with the magic of leg spin – practising to bowl leggies gave me a great insight into how difficult the art is. You could 'roll' the ball out and land in a good area, but to be any good, I instinctively knew the bowler had to really give the ball a tweak. That's where practice came in: lots of it, to achieve consistency of line and the ability to build pressure on the batsman.

With every big match Benaud became more consistent, attaining the line and length needed to apply pressure to the batsmen, with his combination of leg breaks, top-spinners, wrong'uns and flippers. What we didn't know at the time was just how hard Benaud worked on all parts of his game.

As a young man he worked as a journalist, and his working hours allowed him to get to the Sydney Cricket Ground long before the other players arrived for the state squad training. Benaud took advantage by grabbing a bag of balls and heading for the nets at the SCG No 2 Ground. There he would place a handkerchief on a good length and bowl for hours to hit his target, ball after ball after ball. He bowled mainly stock-leg breaks, each with lots of over spin, but at varying paces. Subtle variation it had to be, for only subtle changes in pace can lead to the spinner breaking the rhythm of the batsman. The rhythm of his approach and drive through the crease was paramount, for a spinner must also develop a repeatable action.

Just like the youngsters who half a century later saw Shane Warne in action, the youngsters of my time had every little Benaud idiosyncrasy down pat: one step forward, then five lengthy paces towards the bowling crease, the shirt unbuttoned to the waist, hair slicked down, the pursed lips and thoughtful stare at the batsman after each ball. His bowling was all rhythm and energy. He paradoxically combined a cultivated style with a bold, almost carefree, quest to attack at all costs. Benaud was always turned out immaculately, not a hair out of place, his shirt unbuttoned to reveal a bronzed chest. Every inch a warrior-cricketer, he was always up for the contest. We loved it.

We loved his dashing style, and his admiration of Miller was proof positive to us that heroes also have their heroes. As a youngster in the NSW team, Benaud sat with Miller one day enjoying a cold beer after play, looking over the beautiful Adelaide Oval and to the magnificent St Peter's Cathedral in the distance, behind the iconic scoreboard.

'Gee Nugget, I wish I had been given the chance to bowl to Bradman,' Benaud said, of the greatest batsman of them all.

'Ah, hem,' Miller almost choked in reply, or was he clearing his throat to add authority to his words? 'Son, that you never got to bowl to Bradman was the biggest break you've had in cricket.'

I was watching; I was also reading. There was something magical about reading about the spinners of the past. In the years to come I was blessed to have the chance to get to know two spinners who *did* bowl to Bradman, Clarrie Grimmett and Bill O'Reilly. They were the great spin pair between the wars, and their words introduced me to spinners of the late 19th century.

In 1926 O'Reilly was training with the NSW state squad at the SCG when old Test champion Arthur Mailey suggested he change his grip.

'Thanks for the advice Mr Mailey, but I think I'll stick with this grip. It has served me well since I was young,' said the 20-year-old O'Reilly.

Then to Bill's surprise came a voice from behind the net. 'They tried to change me too, yer know. But I stuck to my guns, same as you.

3

Good on yer, son.' It was none other than CTB Turner, 'the Terror', legendary spinner of the 1880s.

Australia over the years has produced some of the greatest spin bowlers the world has seen – and there is a thread that connects them over the years. We will follow that thread, seeing how the skills and secrets have been passed from one generation of the spin bowling brotherhood to the next. The thread passes from CTB Turner to Mailey to O'Reilly, who Sir Donald Bradman considered the greatest bowler, on through Clarrie Grimmett, arguably the father of spin bowling in Australia and definitely the creator of the flipper, who passed it to Benaud, from whom it eventually made its way to Shane Warne, its greatest exponent and the greatest spinner of them all.

I have drawn on my own experience as a player for Australia, South Australia and Western Australia, and from my years as a coach working with many of the modern spinners including Warne, Tim May and Stuart MacGill, not to mention those who played for countries other than Australia. In addition I have drawn on the batsmen who played the great spinners through the years, while for the ancients I researched widely and spoke to old spinners and batsmen to help me to create the best word pictures of these past champions.

The Magic of Spin will kindle the memories of the old and fire the enthusiasm of the young. Come in, spinners.

Don Bradman with his 'Don Bradman' brand Sykes bat, 1932. (SAM HOOD, COURTESY
OF STATE LIBRARY OF NEW SOUTH WALES)

BEFORE THE
GREAT WAR

Not even Samuel Johnson could have envisioned the impact the game of cricket would have across the world. Dr Johnson derived the word 'cricket' from the Old English word 'cryce'; a stick. The word 'cryce' survives in Devon and Cornwall in the sense of hedge sticks. Pictorial evidence of the game dates back to the 13th century and cricket was played by boys of the Royal Grammar School at Guildford round 1550. Even the Puritan republican Oliver Cromwell is reported as having indulged in cricket in his youth. But the cricket then was a very primitive form of the game, almost unrecognisable to the game we enjoy today.

Cricket fields of yore were chosen according to the shortness of the grass – perhaps thanks to grazing sheep – for the surface had to be fairly flat. Bowlers twisted, twirled and spun their underarm stuff, but usually the ball was trundled all the way along the ground like a jazzed-up version of lawn bowls. The bowler moved in hunched fashion as would a 10 pin bowler, twisting or spinning it to the left (leg spin) or the right (off spin). But the ball travelled all the way along the ground length of the pitch and the batsmen needed long-handled hockey-like bats to sweep the ball away.

More than 200 years before Shane Warne exploded onto the world stage, the merry men of Broad Halfpenny Lane were the champions of Hambledon in Hampshire. Back in the late

18th century the underarm 'master of the Lob', Hambledon spinner 'Lumpy' Stevens, inadvertently bowled a third stump into the game of cricket.

There was spin magic afoot here because Lumpy caused his underarm 'zooter' – a ball later reinvented by Warne – to scoot past the flailing blade of England's then premier batsman, John Small. It was Tuesday 23 May 1775 that Lumpy beat Small, but the ball failed to hit the woodwork. Three times in succession the ball careered past Small's bat and straight through the gap between off stump and leg stump. In those days cricket was played with two stumps and one large bail on top. The set of stumps resembled an upright rectangle. Thanks to Lumpy Stevens a third stump was introduced and the stumps by the early 1800s looked pretty much as they do today.

By the early 1800s batsmen were using a more conventional-looking bat, something akin to those we see today. In the early 19th century the underarm brigade was joined by the 'round armers'.

The underarm twisters and spinners remained until one extraordinary day in the game between Marylebone Cricket Club (MCC) and Kent at Lord's on 15 July 1822 when a certain John Willes, who played a handful of first-class games for Kent, was no-balled for delivering a ball with his arm above the level of his waist. He caught the idea from his sister – her voluminous skirts prevented her from bowling with her arm any lower than her waist in family cricket matches. Sadly Willes was so incensed by his being no-balled for 'unlawful bowling' that he stormed from the field to nearby St John's Wood where his horse was tethered and rode out of the game altogether. It took barely a decade for Willes' method to become legal.

The first recorded cricket match in Australia had taken place in Sydney, probably at the Domain, in December 1803. Contained in a report published in *The Sydney Gazette* on 8 January 1804 was the contention that cricket was already well established in the infant colony. From the turn of the century, certainly by the year 1802, teams made up of Redcoats, whose day job was to guard the convicts, were often pitched against players brought together from all manner of fields: farmers, shopkeepers, bankers, investors. Intercolonial cricket began when a team in Tasmania took on a visiting Victorian XI at Launceston in February 1851 – the Tasmanians winning by three wickets. Then came the first English tour of Australia – HH Stephenson's side – in the summer of 1861–62.

As the game evolved round-arm bowling became the norm and spin was largely side spin. What I would call real bowling did not evolve until over-arm bowling was legalised, in 1864, coincidentally the first year WG Grace began his epic career and the year Wisden published its first *Cricketers' Almanack*. Spinners could now get their wrists in a better position to apply lots of over spin to their leg and off spinners. Underarm bowling was still legal, but as the years went by this practice stopped entirely; that is, until 1981 when Greg Chappell instructed his brother Trevor to bowl underarm to deny New Zealand any chance to smack a six off the last ball to win an ODI match in Melbourne. All hell broke loose; Kiwi Prime Minister Robert 'Piggy' Muldoon and his Australian counterpart Malcolm Fraser condemned this cricketing atrocity. The end result was that the International Cricket Council (ICC) banned underarm bowling forevermore.

Leading up to the Great War Australia was blessed with a number of champion spin bowlers. To discover the best of them was a matter of long and thorough research of newspaper articles from the 19th century and books by authors such as AG 'Johnnie' Moyes, whose *A Century of Cricketers* brought to life many of those featured here. Moyes, a batsman who played for SA and NSW, played against spinners Dr Herbert 'Ranji' Hordern and Monty Noble. Although selected for Australia to tour South Africa in

1914, Moyes never got a chance to represent his country, as the Great War intervened. Moyes gleaned information from Hordern and Noble and also spoke with George Giffen, William 'Farmer Bill' Howell and CTB Turner.

GEORGE GIFFEN

'Australia's WG Grace'

George Giffen was typical of the off-break merchants who operated before the Great War. He delivered the ball at a slow medium pace, blending deadly accurate off-breaks with a clever top-spinner that either went straight on or slightly away from the right-hander. In 1874, at the age of 15 George was invited to bowl to WG Grace's visiting England side. In those days the nets at the Adelaide Oval were on the ground itself. Practice done, a team of groundsmen would dash to the area and dismantle the nets just before the two umpires appeared on the field.

The third son of a carpenter, Giffen was born on 27 March 1859. He began his working life as a postman. He loved the outdoors, so the job suited him perfectly. George loved the outdoors and while he sometimes rode a bicycle, he preferred to walk. It was the beginning of a lifelong habit of fitness. He played Australian Rules football for both Norwood and the state, and although cricket was his favourite sport, his name is forever linked with Norwood football club. The club's original victory song, sung to the tune of 'Killarney', contained these lines:

Giffen, dashing through the fray,
Kicked first goal for Norwood.

He trained assiduously at cricket practice, always bowling for at least two hours. Giffen then ran alone round the boundary line at Adelaide Oval before collecting his gear, tearing up Montefiore Hill at the back of Adelaide Oval and walking home to Norwood. Giffen was a big, fit, strong, square-shouldered man with massive hands. He developed into a WG Grace type of character, in that he dominated the scoresheets and ruled over his peers like a tyrant. He toured England on five occasions – 1882, 1884, 1886, 1893 and 1896. Twice he declined tour invitations (in 1888 and 1890).

Giffen played in the famous one-off Test at The Oval in 1882. There was jiggery-pokery afoot when WG Grace whipped off the bails to run out SP Jones, who had wandered out of his ground to, as he later explained, 'do a bit of gardening and flatten down a lump on the pitch'.

The Australians clearly heard WG's squeaky appeal and Umpire Thoms, standing to attention as if addressing a senior officer on the field, saying out loud: 'As you claim it, sir. Out!'

The Australians were fuming. They believed old WG had done them with a dose of his usual skulduggery, or, as the good doctor might say, 'gamesmanship'.

The Australian second innings closed at a paltry 122, leaving England just 85 runs to win. In his book *With Bat and Ball*, Giffen said Fred Spofforth, the team's demon fast bowler, and other players were incensed. Spofforth strode up and down the dressing-room like a caged lion.

Then he stopped and with a fierce glare he eyeballed every member of the side and said defiantly, 'This thing can be done!'

Spofforth's stirring words fired up his teammates and they dashed down the stairs and onto the field like steely-eyed commandoes going to battle.

Spofforth and Harry Boyle did the bulk of the bowling, but it was the demon fast bowler who did all the damage. Having taken 7/46 in the England first innings, he backed up with 7/44 in the second dig.

More importantly, his prophecy was proved correct: Australia won the Test, by just seven runs.

The Sporting Life published a mock obituary five days after the match ended. It was the work of Reginald Brooks, son of the editor of *Punch*. The jest sparked the legend of The Ashes thus:

In affectionate remembrance

of

English Cricket

Which died at The Oval

on

29th August, 1882

Deeply lamented by a large circle of

Sorrowing friends and Acquaintances

R.I.P.

NB – The body will be cremated and

The Ashes taken to Australia

On the voyage to England on the *Assam*, Giffen wrote of his love of touring and the fellowship of the team. 'Sailing on the bosom of the mighty deep and the rollicking fun, feasting, high jinks and elocution,' he wrote.

Giffen recalled the voyage home in even more glowing terms: 'We were all heroes. Everyone joined in honouring us. When I reached Adelaide I was made the recipient of a chronograph watch and chain valued at 100 guineas.' That was a small fortune at the time.

George Giffen was a giant of the game Down Under. He bestrode Australian cricket like a colossus, especially the domestic game. His greatest performance in Intercolonial cricket was in the 1891–92 summer when he scored 271, then proceeded to take a match haul of 16 wickets to beat Victoria. The noted English writer and historian Harry Altham said Giffen's feat against the Victorians was 'surely the greatest all-round performance in recorded cricket history in any class'.

Giffen was a postal worker for 43 years, retiring with a pension in 1925.

He never married, but after his cricket finished he delighted in coaching youngsters in the South Park Lands opposite his Adelaide home. Each day the boys would be waiting at 6 am and Giffen would take them through their paces until 7.30 am. The boys called themselves the 'early risers'.

In 251 first-class matches Giffen scored 11,757 runs at 29.6. He captured 1022 wickets at 21.31. In 31 Tests he scored 1238 runs at 23.35 and took 103 wickets at 27.09. During his long first-class career Giffen bowled 46,916 balls. Right up until his final years he was fit and strong and he walked everywhere, avoiding catching a train, bus or car whenever he could.

When he was 61 George attended a postal Sunday picnic at Belair National Park in the Adelaide Hills. One of the contests that day was bowling at a single stump. Unbeknown to George, someone put his name down as an entrant. Some competitors hit the single stump once; one hit it on two occasions before George was called from the beer tent. He walked to the pitch, took off his coat and, with that familiar swing of both arms back and high and a sprightly approach of eight paces, he proceed to hit that single stump nine times in a row.

As with all of us, Giffen had his cricketing strengths and weaknesses. His strengths are well documented. His weakness? He loved bowling and as the South Australian captain he could never find a way to take himself out of the attack. Once when wheeling away for hours without much success a teammate dared to ask, 'What do you think about a change, George?'

'Yes, my good man. Good idea. I'll bowl from the other end.'

When Giffen died at the age of 68 in Adelaide on 29 March 1927 after a long illness, fellow test players Joe Darling and Clem Hill eulogised him at his funeral for the willing hours he spent bowling to them and other young players, helping them on their way to international cricketing fame.

CTB TURNER

'The Terror'

The year is 1942 and the world is in the turmoil of war. Arthur Mailey, in his mid fifties, visits 'The Terror' at his home near the beach in Manly and asks him how he managed to get so much turn on the ball.

Old CTB Turner stands from his armchair and walks briskly to the sideboard, picks up an orange and crushes it to a pulp in his fingers.

A young CTB Turner developed that strength on the billiard balls at the grand three-storey, 37-room Royal Hotel in William Street, Bathurst, which his father kept. Charles Thomas Biass Turner used to muck about with the billiard balls, learning to impart vicious spin on them. Having huge hands was an advantage.

He was called 'The Terror' because of his ability to break the ball either way at a speed of around 55 miles per hour, 90 kilometres an hour these days. Most at the time said that was too fast for any bowler to be able to turn the ball, but Turner wasn't just 'any' bowler.

Turner was educated at the Bathurst Grammar School but didn't play in the first XI. Reflecting on his early years Turner said he 'never cared a straw for the game'. But something must have stirred in the boy Turner, because by the time he had reached his teens his cricket was something to behold. He operated with a front-on action and a low arm. Today coaches would frown upon his method. If the bowler is a front-on merchant he must have a high arm. But a low arm Turner had from the outset and he persisted that way throughout his illustrious career.

In the summer of 1881–82, Turner was invited to play for the Twenty-two of Bathurst against Alfred Shaw's England team. Turner proved an immediate sensation, taking 7/33 and 10/36 in the second innings.

Nineteen-year-old Turner, who was at the time working for Cobb & Co, was refused leave by his employer to play in the match. His employer was a hard-nosed businessman, an American named James Rutherford, who may well have thought cricket was a chirping thing in the thicket.

Thankfully fate took a hand.

RJ Black, a member of the Legislative Council in NSW and an avid cricket follower, intervened on Turner's behalf, convincing the American to 'give the boy a go' and allow him time off to play against the Englishmen. According to the *Bathurst Times:*

> Turner's bowling was the feature of the Bathurst side. The uncertain nature of the turf, of course, assisted him, but apart from that he bowled with great accuracy and having once 'got on the spot' he kept it.

It took another year for Turner to be invited to play a state match for NSW. He was an immediate success in the Intercolonial matches and was soon earmarked for Test cricket.

At 19 Charlie married Sarah Emily Matthews. Sarah, always known affectionately as 'Em', was a few years older than CTB. In 1883, Charlie and Em moved to Sydney. He wanted to better himself in the business community, joining the Australian Joint Stock Bank as a clerk.

He had made his state debut for NSW in December 1882. It was not a full strength NSW side as Alick Bannerman, Tom Garrett, Sammy Jones, HH Massie, William Murdoch and Fred Spofforth were still on the high seas sailing home from the England tour that birthed the Ashes.

That first match was none too successful for Charlie. He took 1/76 and scored 4 and 2 against Ivo Bligh's XI, and NSW lost by an innings and 144 runs.

Charlie and Em were a happy couple living in Sydney. At his work with the bank Charlie had 'obtained considerable promotion' and was 'assiduous in the discharge of his duties'. But tragedy struck the Turner family in December 1883. Em, heavily pregnant, was in delicate health and died of an 'unnatural childbirth' on 9 December 1883. Their child, a son, was stillborn.

He was just 21 when Em died. Charlie was to marry again – twice.

Turner made his Test debut against England at the SCG in January 1887. He took 6/15 in the England first dig off 18 overs and 2/53 in the England second innings. John James (JJ) Ferris, the left-armer who swung and spun at medium pace, also debuted in that game, collecting 9/103 in the match.

Australia lost the game by 13 runs, but Turner and 'Jack' Ferris forged a brilliant bowling partnership from that match onward.

Turner took a record 106 wickets in 12 matches in the Australian season of 1887–88, still a record for any bowler in an Australian season. That clinched his selection for the 1888 Australian tour of England, the first of his three tours to the 'Old Country'. In 1888 the team played some 40 first-class matches. In those days the players got a share of the gate, so the more games they played the better the money. He took an incredible 283 wickets at 11.27 runs apiece in the first-class games in England in 1888. In all matches he took 314 wickets.

Charlie Turner and Jack Ferris took an incredible 482 wickets between them on that 1888 tour.

Charlie Turner had a simple bowling philosophy. He said at the peak of his career:

> I always go for the wickets more than bowling for catches. In bowling I have always made it a point to commence to a new man with a view of finding his weak points and then go for him with a 'break'. But I look on bowling as a 'gift' or knack. Some men have all the attributes – strength, robustness, having all the nerve about them, are healthy and possess a true eye, but they are not bowlers and never will be. There is a gift which I cannot explain, but it is there all the time for the true bowler.

Turner toured England again in 1890, taking 215 wickets at 12.67, and in 1893 capturing 149 wickets at 14.25, although he said the last of his three tours in 1893 was 'the most unpleasant and unsatisfactory trip to the old country that I have ever undertaken'. The Terror singled out the South Australian all-rounder George Giffen as 'a difficult man. When a man is too conceited and plays for himself instead of his side he does a lot of harm.'

The 1894–95 Test series against England was his last in big cricket. With the series tied at 2–2 coming into the decisive fifth Test in Melbourne, Turner was dropped, despite having taken 3/18 and 4/33 in the preceding Test. At the time the top players were the selectors, and Turner was one of them – but he was overruled by his two fellow selectors, George Giffen and Jack Blackham. The cricket world was in shock.

Without Turner, Australia lost the final Test and the series. Sadly Turner never played for Australia again. *Sporting Life* once wrote a typical Turner victim had been 'skittled by a sonnet', reflecting the opinion of England captain Archie MacLaren, who described Turner's bowling as 'poetry in motion'.

Sir Stanley Jackson, the English Test player known as 'the Honourable Stanley Jackson' because he was a member of Parliament, wrote: 'I always regarded Charles Turner as the best medium-paced bowler I ever played against.'

His bowling figures suggest as much. He played 17 Tests for a return of 101 wickets at 16.53. In 155 first-class matches he took 993 wickets at 14.25.

In 2012 Ric Sissons wrote a splendid book on Turner, *The Terror*, with a foreword by Australian Test all-rounder Alan Davidson, who wrote:

> As a young boy falling in love with the game, I was never in doubt about the game's obligations to all those who came before us. In my own time on the field and in the administration of the game in the following five decades, I sought to build awareness of those who made cricket our pre-eminent sport. Charlie [Turner] belongs in my list of all-time greats.

Turner died at the age of 81 in Manly in 1944. Sixty years later the South Australian Cricket Association commissioned a statue of George Giffen at Adelaide Oval. The Terror might have raised an eyebrow at that administrative decision.

DR HV HORDERN

Our first doctor of spin

Herbert Vivian Hordern was born in North Sydney on 10 February 1883. He became the first genuine wrist spinner Australia produced, although because of his work as a dentist his opportunities in world cricket were limited and he played only seven Test matches. But what an impact he made in those few games.

His nickname was 'Ranji' because of his swarthy complexion, believed to be a reference to the famous Indian-born England batsman KS Ranjitsinhji.

Hordern made his first-class debut for NSW in December 1905 taking 8/81 and a total of 11 wickets for the match against Queensland. Then, like a meteor hurtling across the night sky, he was gone. Hordern was set upon pursuing his dentistry studies. He moved to the US, where he studied dentistry at the University of Pennsylvania. But cricket was never far away. In 1908 he toured England with the Philadelphian cricket team, which represented that state from the club's inception in 1878 to 1913, when it was curtailed by the outbreak of the Great War. The team comprised players from the four main cricket clubs in Philadelphia – Germantown, Merion, Belmont and Philadelphia – and rivalled many others in the world. Philadelphia often toured England and played against the counties and minor teams. It was in Philadelphia that Hordern got the opportunity to play a good standard of cricket, touring England during his study breaks. The team played 88 first-class matches over its 35 years of existence, for 29 wins, 45 losses, 13 draws and one abandoned.

It was in England that Hordern became interested in the possibilities of delivering an off-break with a seeming leg-break action. The Englishman Bernard Bosanquet first hit on the idea and is acknowledged as the creator of the delivery. Thus the ball was called a 'Bosey'. Bosanquet read an article in an English magazine about a fellow who was bowling leg breaks on the beach in the UK. The man gradually wore a hole in the sand, for he consistently landed his front foot on the same spot. Nothing unusual in that; however, when the hole became deeper, the fellow's shoulder dropped and instead of bowling leg breaks, the ball turned in the opposite direction, spinning from the off toward leg. His shoulder had dropped to such an extent because of the front foot landing in the deep hole that the ball was delivered out of the back of the hand and not over the wrist as is the norm for the leg break. Bosanquet was curious, so he experimented alone for hours and came up with the Bosey. He had no idea that the delivery was the spinning equivalent of inventing the wheel.

Nowadays in Australia the ball is known as a 'wrong'un' and in England and elsewhere it is called a 'googly'.

One day during a break in play during a rainstorm Hordern experimented with a tennis ball. He spun the ball on to saucers on the tea table and discovered that by dropping his wrist and bowling out of the back of his hand the ball spun in the air exactly as would an off-break.

It then dawned on him that the leg break is always an over-the-wrist action; the Bosey is always a back-of-the-hand action. Buoyed by his success in a number of matches, he decided to put his new method into action. In one match against a strong MCC team at Lord's, Hordern took 8/31.

Hordern played 17 first-class matches for the Philadelphians, perfecting his wrong'un. Soon after his return to Australia in 1910, the NSW and Australian left-handed opening batsman Warren Bardsley convinced Hordern that he must show Australia his amazing skills by making himself available to play state cricket. In the wake of taking 43 wickets in six games for NSW, Hordern was selected to play in the fourth Test against South Africa, at the Melbourne Cricket Ground (MCG), taking 3/39 and 5/66. Curiously in the fifth Test, at the SCG, Hordern batted No 3 and Victor Trumper down the list, despite Hordern not having distinguished himself at No 9 in the previous Test. Hordern hit 50 and Trumper 31, but the great Trumper was back at No 3 in the second dig, hitting an unconquered 74 to ensure an Australian victory by seven wickets. Hordern took 4/73 and 2/117 in that game to complete a haul of 14 wickets for 295 at an average of 21.07.

His Test series spinning pièce de résistance came the next season when he played a full Ashes series, taking 32 wickets at 24.37, including four bags of five wickets or more; his 5/85 and 7/90 against England in the first Test at Sydney confirming his status as the most remarkable and talented leg spinner Australia had produced. His wrong'un was said to have been the most potent and lethal delivery. He captured the wicket of the great Jack Hobbs five times during the series.

AG 'Johnnie' Moyes, one of the best batsmen in Australia from about 1910 to the Great War, was a journalist and author and keen observer of the game, who saw all the great leg spinners before the

Great War and all of them between the wars. He believed Hordern to be the best of his tribe.

'Hordern took a longer run than most of his type, but it was smooth, not jerky like Grimmett's, or casual like Mailey's,' he wrote.

> In type he approximated more to the Grimmett school. He was a length bowler as well as a spinner. Unlike Mailey he never invited a batsman's contempt. His extra inches gave him an advantage over Grimmett as far as flighting the ball was concerned.
>
> He turned the ball about the same amount as Clarrie, but less than Mailey. His disguise was excellent. The only visible sign – and you needed good eyesight – was the tip of the little finger pointing skyward as he dropped his wrist to bowl the 'Bosey'.

Moyes thought Hordern of the same stature as Mailey and Grimmett.

> On Australian wickets he was as good as Mailey and better than Grimmett; in England he would, I think, have been as outstanding as Clarrie. With his control of length, his ability to flight the ball and his clever fingers, I don't see how he could have failed.

That, however, we will never know; Hordern made himself unavailable for the 1912 tour of England, a tour in which England, Australia and South Africa played a triangular Test series. But he did make himself available for Victor Trumper's benefit match at the SCG in 1913, in which Johnnie Moyes also played.

The fleet-footed Trumper told Moyes that he never tried to pick the break. 'If you can get out to the ball, it doesn't matter. If you can't, then go back again; it doesn't matter.' That theory is fine – if you are fast enough on your feet. I remember the great South African Barry

Richards had the same idea when facing the finger-flick 'mystery' of John Gleeson in the 1970s.

Moyes tried the theory. Down the track he went to Hordern in the Trumper Benefit game, misread the wrong'un – and the ball careered through the gap between bat and pad for Sammy Carter to complete the stumping: '"Beat you, son." And out I went.'

The Trumper Benefit Match was one of Hordern's last first-class matches. He served in the Australian Imperial Force (AIF) in the Middle East, then upon his return to Australia he settled back into a career in dentistry before working as a stockbroker. In just 35 first-class matches Hordern took 228 wickets at 16.36 with his best the 8/31 for Philadelphians against MCC at Lord's in 1908. In seven Test matches he took 46 wickets at 23.36 with five hauls of five wickets in an innings and twice taking 10 or more wickets in a match.

Hordern was the first of the great leg spinners. Had he played more cricket, allowing more eyes to see him and more tongues to extol his virtues, he might well have been discussed alongside Mailey, Grimmett, O'Reilly and Warne as the greatest of their tribe.

BILL HOWELL

'What a buzz'

Born in Penrith, Sydney, on 29 December 1869, Bill Howell played 18 Tests from 1898 to 1904. He was among those bowlers before the Great War who bowled a steady medium pace, but spun the ball from the off to fool the batsman. Howell was from a family of beekeepers in the district of Rooty Hill, NSW – and boy, could he make a cricket ball buzz. Life and work on the farm helped him develop immensely strong fingers, 'all the better to spin you out'. 'Farmer Bill' Howell played his first Test on the Adelaide Oval in January 1898. He toured England three times – 1899, 1902 and 1905 – but had the misfortune of playing at the same time as the great Hugh Trumble, so his opportunities were limited. Apart from viciously turning off-breaks, Farmer Bill could also bowl a decent leg break with enough pace to prevent even the most fleet-footed of batsmen getting down the track to drive him.

In 1899, in his first appearance in England, he took all 10 Surrey wickets at The Oval – which was two wickets more than he took in the five Tests that followed.

Bill Howell poses for the camera. (ASHLEY MALLETT COLLECTION)

A strongly built farm lad sporting a huge handlebar moustache, Howell used flight and pace to defeat the batsman in the air. He managed to gain enormous purchase on the ball and spun it a treat. The snap of Howell's strong fingers caused the ball to fizz loudly on its way towards the batsman.

In the two Tests he played in South Africa in 1902 – played not on turf but on coir matting pitches – Howell took 14 wickets at 12.42, ensuring success for the Australians. He opened the bowling in both innings of the third Test. In 1904 Bill finished his career with NSW. He took 521 first-class wickets at an average of 21.45. His 49 Test wickets cost 28.71. Had he played before or after Trumble those figures would have been even better. After his cricket career ended Farmer Bill went back to his bees on one of the family farms in the Rooty Hill area.

HUGH TRUMBLE

'Is circus in town?'

The great English cricketer and all-round athlete CB Fry said of Hugh Trumble: 'You were up against a brain as well as an arm.'

Born in Abbotsford, a Melbourne inner suburb, on 19 May 1867, Hugh was the third son of William Trumble, who hailed from Northern Ireland, and Elizabeth Clark.

Hugh's father was a civil servant and he bowled leg breaks for South Melbourne. He later laid a turf wicket on his property where the family had moved, on the edge of the Yarra River in Kew, and taught his four sons the rudiments of spin bowling. The Trumble boys' dad placed a feather on a good length and encouraged them to aim at it. He wanted to see 'good line and length'.

Hugh quickly came up through the ranks. In the summer of 1889–90 Trumble, aged 22, was playing for Victoria and couldn't break through against NSW. He believed that his chances of making the Australian team for its coming tour of England in 1890 were dwindling.

To lift his spirits over lunch a friend suggested he try a cold beer as a 'refreshing, energising' pathway to a bag of wickets. It was Trumble's first go at the amber liquid and he liked it straight away. He drank a few more before the players went back on the field. His anxiety gone, Trumble bowled beautifully after the lunch adjournment, taking a bundle of wickets at low cost and ensuring his spot on the England tour. At the age of 23 Trumble played his first Test at Lord's but with the two old campaigners – CTB Turner and JJ (Jack) Ferris – in the side, he was given only a handful of overs in that match and in the other Test he played on the tour.

Against Sheffield at Bramall Lane as the players took the field, spectators formed a lane through which the players walked. Trumble was 193 centimetres tall – to the spectators, 6 feet 3 inches – which is to say, he was very tall for a man in the late 1800s. The onlookers gaped at the tall, angular Australian with the huge drooping moustache. He looked nothing like a cricketer. One wag yelled in a broad Yorkshire accent: 'Is circus in town?'

Then from the aisle came the command, 'Stand oop, tha long coot, and let's ha' look at thee.'

They loved looking at him. Monty Noble loved watching Trumble bowl. He described the long fellow's approach to the wicket as 'sidelong and insinuating, with his neck craned like a gigantic bird'. A pterodactyl comes to mind or the Concorde supersonic aircraft, each with craned 'neck' lowered to spy a clear place to land.

Trumble fielded at first slip to the likes of Turner and Giffen. He possessed long, slender fingers and could catch anything at slip – a fly twixt forefinger and thumb, any nick from a bowler within reach. He was the first fieldsman to take 20 catches or more in an Australian first-class season and England's Johnny Douglas complained that Trumble should never be allowed on a cricket field because his place was 'scampering up trees in the bush'.

On his third England tour, in 1896, Trumble took the most wickets (148) for the Australians and was named among *Wisden's* Five Cricketers of the Year.

Off-spinner Hugh Trumble on the 1899 Australian tour of England. (ASHLEY
MALLETT COLLECTION)

That season he went to Lord's to watch the annual match between Eton and Harrow. Hugh sat in front of an old Etonian, who continually voiced his opinion about bowling changes, field placements and sundry matters, punctuating his furious attack on all and sundry on the fielding side by thumping Trumble on the back. Tired of being hit, Trumble started to disagree with some of the old Etonian's opinions.

This caused the man to lean forward and say, 'Excuse me, sir. I don't know who you are but it is evident you know nothing whatsoever about the game of cricket.' Hugh smiled and looked straight ahead. At least the thumps on his back stopped while the man's tirade continued unabated.

Trumble used his great height to create what many thought to be a confusing flight path. He learned to hold one back. Batsmen were often trapped into thinking the ball was a gentle half volley, when, in fact, the ball suddenly dipped and they spooned a catch, either to a fielder or the bowler, who covered a lot of ground.

England's Sir Stanley Jackson was more than once hoodwinked by Trumble's slower ball, which he spooned back to the bowler. 'You old devil, Hughie,' he used to laugh, 'but I'll pick that slower one sooner or later!'

Trumble was said to have been a master of deceit. He could spin the ball a lot, but his clever brain told him that a little turn is a dangerous thing. Trumble bowled to hit the stumps or hit the pads in front of the stumps. He wanted batsmen to play the ball with their bat not merely pad the ball away. There was an enduring relentlessness about his bowling. No batsman ever really belted him. Ball after ball, Trumble kept at the batsman. While his control was remarkable, he always sought to vary his pace. In the 1901–02 Australian summer Trumble took 28 wickets and in England shortly thereafter came a 26-wicket haul against England on their home soil.

Australian cricket writer Ray Robinson wrote of Trumble: 'El Greco with his lengthening touch would have liked to draw Trumble. Hugh's lantern-shaped head set on a column of a neck would have given the Spaniard a halfway start.'

Trumble's long face, lantern jaw, prominent ears and large nose combined to become a cartoonist's delight.

WG Grace was full of praise for Trumble: 'The best bowler Australia has sent us.' On board ship to and fro an Ashes tour, Trumble was popular with all and sundry. He loved playing practical jokes. He coached fellow travellers to play quoits.

Accepting Trumble's advice they were made to contort themselves into a number of ludicrous positions, to the great amusement of his teammates. To prolong the joke, the gangling Trumble would adopt the same peculiar stance.

In first-class cricket Trumble scored 5395 runs at 19.47 and took 929 wickets at 18.44 runs apiece. In Tests he scored 851 runs at 19.79 and took 141 wickets at 21.78.

On 4 March 1904 Trumble took 7/28 – including a hat-trick, the second of his Test career – against England at the MCG and promptly retired from international cricket, 14 years after his first Test.

As AG 'Johnnie' Moyes wrote: 'No artist in any walk of life has made a more impressive farewell.'

When not playing cricket Trumble worked in a bank, then in 1911 he was appointed secretary of the Melbourne Cricket Club. An imposing figure in his three-piece suit, complete with serge and watch chain, Trumble always wore a hat with a very broad brim, making him stand out even in a big MCG crowd. He held that post for 27 years, until his death in 1938.

MONTY NOBLE

He knew what he wanted

It was at the MCG on New Year's Day 1902 that Monty Noble achieved his best Test match figures. Bowling in tandem with Hugh Trumble on a typical Melbourne 'sticky dog', as a nasty wet wicket was known, Noble made the ball bite savagely. He held the ball in a strange fashion for a medium-paced off spinner, twixt forefinger and thumb. Indeed an odd grip for a man so set in what were then orthodox methods.

Born Montague Alfred Noble in Sydney's Chinatown on 28 January 1873, Noble was destined to extract batsmen from the crease – and teeth too.

Monty attended the Crown Street Superior School and was just about finishing his schooling when Victor Trumper, some four years his junior, began his education at the same school. Noble's first big break in cricket came aged 21 in the summer of 1894–95 when he was chosen in the NSW Colts team to play Andrew Stoddart's visiting England XI.

Coincidentally Victor Trumper, aged 17, was also chosen and the pair put on quite a show, Noble with a sometimes stubborn, sometimes brilliant 152 not out and Trumper with an ever dashing 67.

After first working for a bank, the young Noble left when his employer refused to grant him leave to play cricket. By the 1897–98 season Noble was established in the NSW team. He was first picked to play for Australia against England at the MCG that summer. In Australia's first innings of 520, Noble scored a modest 17. Then he took 1/31 off 12 promising overs in England's first innings.

When England batted again Noble bowled in tandem with Hugh Trumble and the pair went to town – Noble taking 6/49 and Trumble 4/53. Australia won handsomely, by an innings and 55 runs.

Australian all-rounder Monty Noble enjoys a rest aboard the *SS Ormuz*, bound for England with the 1899 Australians. (ASHLEY MALLETT COLLECTION)

Soon enough Noble was being touted for Australia's 1899 team bound for England. While he waited expectantly for news of the make-up of the team he studied dentistry at Sydney University.

Noble's decision to leave banking and become a dentist was an indication of the man's belief. He figured that running his own business would allow him ample time off to play cricket internationally. And playing top cricket in those days meant plenty of tours abroad, mainly the UK to battle the old enemy, England. And just as Dr WG Grace called in a locum to attend to business while he was away, Noble reckoned he would call upon a dental colleague to do the same. Noble did tour England in 1899, so too Trumper. In fact the first Test at Nottingham was WG Grace's last Test and Trumper's first. In the first innings Noble had old WG caught behind for 28 and in the second innings Bill Howell bowled him for 1. It was the end of an era and the start of a new exciting one.

Noble toured England again in 1902 under the captaincy of Joe Darling. Australia easily won the 1902–03 series against South Africa and, in the wake of Darling retiring from the game, Noble took over the Australian captaincy. His debut was an initiation by fire.

He rescued the Australian first innings in the first Test against England in 1903–04 with a sound, patient 133 when the champions around him failed dismally: Trumper (1), Clem Hill (5) and Reg Duff (3) all fell early. Australia managed just 285; England replied with 577, Reg Foster hitting a career-best 287 on debut, which remained the highest Test score by a batsman visiting these shores for the next 111 years.

Australia was well placed in the second innings to make a real fist of things with Trumper and Hill in total command. After hitting three fours, Trumper thumped a ball down the ground and the pair scampered three, and they tried to run two more on an overthrow. Hill looked to have made his ground, but umpire Bob Crockett raised his index finger and Hill was run out for 51. Hill believed he had made his ground easily. He didn't argue, but he did show his annoyance by thumping his pad with his bat. As he walked off he looked up at the heavens, as if to say, 'Why me?', shrugged his shoulders and continued along his way to the pavilion.

The crowd was incensed. There was a very loud and angry chant of 'Crock, Crock, Crock!' as well as booing and hissing as Hill walked disconsolately towards the gate. The England captain Pelham 'Plum' Warner was upset, even more so when he realised that much of the hissing and catcalls emanated from the members' stand. He tried to restrain the booing, but instead it intensified. He unwittingly incited a riot. Noble joined Trumper at the crease and the three cricketers sat on the grass on the edge of the cut portion of the pitch waiting for order to be restored. Warner spoke first: 'If this anger by the crowd doesn't stop I shall be compelled to take my men off the field.' Noble assured him that the crowd would soon come to their senses. The noise abated and the game continued, but as soon as the first ball was bowled the crowd renewed their displeasure.

'How much did you pay Crockett, Warner?'

'Have you got your coffin ready?"

'What gate are you leaving by, Crockett?'

Sir William McKell, who was to become a NSW Labor premier and then Governor-General, was at the ground that day.

'I vividly recall the day,' he told me back in the mid 1980s. He was 93 then, but sharp as a tack.

Clem Hill was clearly in, but he was given out and the crowd heckled. Funny, really. It wasn't as bad as Warner made out. A fellow standing next to me accidentally dropped a bottle of beer – an empty one – and it fell down onto the cycle track which surrounded the SCG in those days. It made a crazy tinkling noise as it rolled down the track and everyone cheered. Others followed suit and soon there were hundreds of bottles being rolled down the incline. The heckling stopped, common sense prevailed; from then on only cheering.

Trumper went on to score a brilliant 185 not out; Hill had fallen foul at 51, Noble hit 27 after a first innings century and Jack Gregory hit grandly for 43. Australia scored 477, but it wasn't enough and England scored the necessary 194 runs to complete a five-wicket victory, eventually taking the series 3–2.

In December 1904 Noble was in his dental surgery when a little man with big ideas nervously entered.

That little man was Bill 'Fergie' Ferguson, a 24-year-old clerk with the Sydney Directory, a precursor to the phone book, listing the city's businesses. Ferguson was looking for adventure – and what better way to see the world than to travel it with the Australian cricket team.

Fergie figured that a formal application to be the team scorer to the team manager Frank Laver would not do, so he decided to take his dream to the dentist captain, who was about to make a decision that would reverberate for almost half a century.

'I have known men, to all intents and purposes masters of their own destiny, fearless and upstanding, blanch, quake and quiver at the very thought of a visit to the surgery for dental treatment,' Fergie wrote years later in his book *Mr Cricket*.

No fillings were required, but Fergie booked a few visits anyway, and got to know Noble pretty well. When Noble wasn't tinkering with his teeth, Fergie got in a few words and talked of his dream to travel the world with the cricket team as its scorer–cum–baggage man.

One day Noble said: 'There is no reason in the world why you shouldn't get the job.'

But the side left Australia en route to England via New Zealand and Canada without him. Fergie was crestfallen. The team had decided to appoint an Englishman when they docked in the UK. Then a letter arrived that 'changed my whole life', he later wrote.

Dated February 1905, it was written on ship notepaper – the SS *Manuka* – at sea near Auckland. Fergie was offered the job at a salary of £2 a week plus train fares to the various grounds for matches.

'The engagement begins from the date of our first match in England and will last, as long as you give satisfaction, until the completion of the tour in England.'

Fergie proved a very popular figure. His career with the Australians began in 1905 and ended with a tour of South Africa with New Zealand in 1953–54. He created the 'wagon wheel' – that distinctive cricket image of the batsman's scoring shots marked on paper emanating from the centre. Fergie made every tour of England from 1905 to 1953, and also worked for England, South Africa and New Zealand teams. Fergie travelled the world, alright, thanks to a dentist-cum-cricketer named Monty Noble – and returned the favour.

In 1913 he recommended his sister Elizabeth Ellen Ferguson to have her teeth checked by Noble. A year later Monty and Elizabeth were married. They produced four children. Monty Noble was a home-loving soul, with what was described as a 'pleasant singing voice', a product of church choir training. Monty loved to ring church bells and when on tour in England he would check out the bells in dozens of old churches. He died in 1940 at the age of 67.

The Noble Stand at the SCG bears his name to this day, and it was there at the second Ashes Test of 1954–55, when I saw Test cricket for the first time, sitting on the fence with my grandfather, Pop, as Frank Tyson bowled his thunderbolts and Neil Harvey carved up the England attack.

Noble played 42 Tests scoring 1997 runs (highest score 133) at an average of 30.25. He took 121 wickets at 25 with a best of 7/17.

Monty was a staunch believer in his players and took their side in disputes with the cricket authorities. He continued his association with cricket, especially the Paddington club in Sydney where it all began for him, and he became a broadcaster and author of three important books: *The Game's the Thing*, *Gilligan's Men* and *Those Ashes*. At the time of his death he was a member of the Sydney Cricket Ground Trust.

Noble was one of Australia's first great all-round cricketers. He was also a splendid captain, shrewd, calm, consistent. Monty Noble knew what he wanted in life and went for it.

BETWEEN
THE WARS

When the guns of the Great War fell silent, cricket was again on the minds of young, competitive cricketers. If you were any good you could play for your country and tour abroad. This was always the case, but travel was becoming more reliable, communication more sophisticated and arguably the standard of spin bowling was getting better. Warwick Armstrong and Arthur Mailey were champions before the war, but their impact on the game was immense from the 1920–21 summer until they hung up their boots.

The Great War was, at risk of understatement, a time of great suffering. The Great Depression that followed was too. Distraught families scrimped and scraped, as men failed to find employment. During the dark period of the nation embraced a cricketer, Don Bradman and a racehorse, Phar Lap, for consolation. Bradman was to take England by storm in 1930, including a Test world record score of 334 at Leeds. The big red New Zealand horse, Phar Lap, stirred the Australian sporting heart by winning both the 1930 Caulfield and Melbourne cups. Another New Zealander was taken to the nation's bosom – leg spinner Clarrie Grimmett. Their feats provided consolation, escape and hope. At the end of that tour, when their fame was at fever pitch, Bradman and Grimmett were each offered £500 to give batting and bowling demonstrations at the London Palladium, 14 performances of at least 10 minutes by each man. I obtained a copy of their contract from Clarrie's son Vic and a few years ago donated it to form part of the CV Grimmett collection at the Wellington Cricket Museum at Basin Reserve in New Zealand. It was an unimaginable sum for those days.

Then along came Bill O'Reilly, the leg spinner they called 'Tiger', the bowler Bradman dubbed the greatest he faced. There were others, of course, such as Don Blackie, who made his Test debut for Australia at the age of 46, Bert Ironmonger, who was so clumsy they called him 'Dainty' and Leslie 'Chuck' Fleetwood-Smith, the 'Chinaman' bowler who spun the cover off the ball. I gleaned much from speaking with Grimmett, O'Reilly and Bradman about the relative merits of the bowlers of the era. Apart from speaking with some of those on my chosen list for this section of the book, I read avidly and talked to some of the batsmen who batted against them; namely England's Frank Woolley, Len Hutton, Bill Edrich and Denis Compton and Australia's Bradman, Keith Miller, Bill Brown, Len Darling and Vic Richardson.

WARWICK ARMSTRONG

'The Big Ship'

Warwick Armstrong was an immense figure in Australian cricket. He went on three England tours – 1902, 1905 and 1909 – with Australia before the Great War, and after it he led Australia there in 1921. It was the impact he made as Australian captain in the summer of 1920–21 and in England 1921 that he will be remembered for most as a cricketer – and those who see his enormous shirt, trousers and boots at the MCG's sport museum will never forget them.

In 1902 Armstrong was a tall, lithe young man of 23, full of enthusiasm and all-round skill. He was rubbing shoulders with the likes of Victor Trumper and Clem Hill in Joe Darling's famous side. At the time Armstrong was a slender 9 stone (57 kilograms); pretty much an elongated stick figure. By 1921 Armstrong had become the 'Big Ship', weighing in at a colossal 21 stone (133 kilograms).

Warwick Windridge Armstrong was born on 22 May 1879, at Kyneton, a country town some 80 kilometres north-west of Melbourne. Educated at Cumloden School, then later at University

College, Armadale, Armstrong at 19 was playing football for South Melbourne in the Victorian Football League (VFL). At 20 his preferred sport was cricket and he joined the Melbourne Cricket Club. He scored a century in his first game for the Victorian XI and in his first Test match against England at the MCG Armstrong was undismissed, getting 4 not out and 45 not out, helping Reg Duff (104) in resurrecting the Australian second innings, thus paving the way for a stirring 225-run victory.

On 12 April 1912 the world mourned the death of a grand lady – the *Titanic*. That was one big ship thought to be unsinkable, unbeatable. By that fateful day Syd Gregory's Australian team was on its own ship, sailing to England, without six of its leading players: Victor Trumper, Clem Hill, Vernon Ransford, Albert 'Tibby' Cotter, Hanson 'Sammy' Carter and Big Ship Armstrong. The 1912 Australian tour of England was to be Australia's most ambitious, a triangular Test series with South Africa the third team.

Three of Australia's greatest cricketers: (from left) Clem Hill, Warwick Armstrong and Victor Trumper, dressed to the nines having breakfast in their London hotel in 1902. (PHOTO BY POPPERFOTO VIA GETTY IMAGES/GETTY IMAGES)

Without the Big Six Australia's chances were thought to be dismal indeed. An argument had erupted between the players and the Board over the appointment of Queenslander GS Crouch as manager when the players wanted Frank Laver, a man they trusted and whom they believed did such a good job as manager on the previous tour in 1909. Letters were exchanged between the Big Six and the Board.

The protesting players were keen to make the tour but not without Laver as manager. Sydney Smith, the Board secretary, wrote a sickly sweet letter to the players scotching all chance of their making the tour unless they fell into line.

> The Board is anxious at all times to send the best team possible, still, at the same time I am sure it will not permit any number of cricketers to dictate the terms and conditions on which a visit is to be made, or if a manager is appointed the terms and nature of his engagement.

Sadly, Trumper never again toured England. He died in 1915, of Bright's disease, which would today be called a diabetic kidney disease. Some quarter of a million people turned out for his Sydney funeral. Nor did Cotter ever get another chance – he was killed in the Middle East during the Great War – but Ransford and Armstrong were to return to big cricket after the war ended, with the Big Ship captain of the 1921 tour, which was again beset by administrative strife.

As captain of the 1921 side Armstrong was concerned by the itinerary set by the Australian Board of Control for International Cricket. The Board had allowed no rest days before three of the scheduled Tests, but Armstrong convinced the Board and a few of the English counties to drop the third day of their matches to allow the Australians to travel to the next Test venue with a day to spare, letting their bowlers recover.

Yorkshire refused, as they felt it would 'belittle the county'. However, eventually Yorkshire agreed to an early start on the third day and the drawing of stumps at 4 pm, thus allowing the team to reach Manchester at 7 pm on the eve of the Test match.

At an Imperial Cricket Conference Armstrong suggested that the umpires not be appointed until the morning of the Test. Legendary MCC administrator Lord Harris asked Armstrong to explain.

'The umpires are paid very little and there is a lot of betting on cricket. It would be wise to remove them from temptation.'

Lord Harris made enquiries and told Armstrong, 'I can find no evidence of betting on cricket – people don't do it.'

'Don't you think so, my Lord? If you'd like £500 on the next Test I can get it for you.'

Armstrong led his men to a 5–0 whitewash in the first post-war Ashes series in 1920–21, then a 3–0 win away in the five-match series of 1921. But he never quite shrugged off the stigma surrounding the 1912 dispute.

On the outward voyage in 1921 Armstrong shovelled coal in the boiler room a few days a week in an attempt to reduce his weight. When the ship left Australia Armstrong was a hefty 21 stone. When it arrived in England he had ballooned out to 22 stone.

By the last day of the fifth Test at The Oval, the game was heading for a tame draw, the Ashes safely retained. As the game wore down, Armstrong placed himself in the outfield. He picked up a discarded newspaper and as the game continued he was seen standing, legs astride, reading the paper. When quizzed by a journalist later about what he was reading, Armstrong laughed, 'To see who we were playing.'

Armstrong was very much his own man. He could be rude – to his players, the opposition and administrators – and when the mood took him, he could be the epitome of good manners and charm. Once during the Melbourne Test of 1920–21 Australia was in trouble and there in the Members' Bar was the Australian captain, padded up as next man in standing with a few of his mates downing a few whiskies. A few minutes later the next wicket fell and out strode the Big Ship. He drove the England bowlers mad with his hefty clouts and finished the innings with a match-winning 158.

Armstrong was indefatigable as a spinner. He bowled small turning leg breaks and top-spinners, but could maintain consistency over long periods. For a huge man his stamina and accuracy was remarkable. He was also said to be remarkably light on his feet for his size, although when he fell on the cricket field he floundered about like a beached whale.

In 50 Tests he hit 2863 runs at 38.68 and took 87 wickets at 33.59.

In first-class cricket Armstrong scored 16,158 runs at 46.83 and took 832 wickets at 19–71.

Armstrong was some mix: cantankerous, a man of strong opinions, a disciplinarian and a mighty hitter of a cricket ball.

His teammates loved, respected and probably feared him.

In 1935 he became general manager for James Buchanan's Whisky.

At the age of 34 he married Aileen O'Donnell, 21, the tiny daughter of a rich Gundagai grazier. They produced a son, who was never destined to become a cricketer. He preferred to swim. Armstrong was a widower when he died on 13 July 1947. His business interests and a good salary at James Buchanan's Whisky proved kind financially. The Big Ship didn't drink all the profits, for he left an estate worth £100,000.

ARTHUR MAILEY

'The Boy Who Killed a Dove'

Arthur Mailey was dubbed 'The Millionaire' for his carefree attitude towards the runs he 'gave' away; by contrast, Clarrie Grimmett was 'The Miser'.

Mailey spun his leg breaks like a top. The ball fairly buzzed out of his hand. It might land on a dangerous length or it might reach the batsman on the full pitch; either way the batsman had no idea what to expect, other than the unexpected.

Mailey began his working life as a labourer; later he excelled as a writer on the game, a cartoonist, an artist, painting in oils and, finally, a butcher.

Emblazoned across the front window of his butcher's shop at Burraneer Bay, south of Sydney, were the words 'I bowled tripe, I wrote tripe and now I sell tripe.'

There was no cricketer, no sporting tradition, in Mailey's impoverished family. He described himself as 'that slum kid'. He picked up the game from playing alongside the local kids in the slum suburb laneways, near the family's tiny wooden house in Sydney's Zetland. He hung a large picture of Victor Trumper, Australia's greatest batting hero before Bradman, on his hessian bagging wall, and when the wind blew gently the hessian danced in the breeze and the image of the famous Trumper drive seemed to come alive.

Born in 1888, Mailey left Waterloo Public School at the age of 13. In 1901 Trumper was at his zenith and all the cricket-mad boys followed their hero to grade and state matches. Sometimes as a special treat they got to watch Trumper in a Test at the SCG.

After the Great War, Mailey played his first Test series for Australia against England, in 1920. By then he was at the top of his powers, taking 36 wickets at 26.27 in the five Tests, including 9/121 in the second innings of the Melbourne fourth Test.

True to his mantle as a millionaire bowler, Mailey was always prepared to exchange runs for wickets. The great England all-rounder Wilfred Rhodes said of him:

> He never gave up. He was sometimes expensive, prepared to buy a wicket but that attitude buoyed his resolve and he might have nought for 100 and finish with six for 130.

The Mailey family loved the royals and Arthur had no hesitation in calling Australians 'we Britishers'. When he retired from cricket Mailey concentrated on writing for the newspapers and, when time allowed, his penchant to paint in oils. In those lazy, hazy days of long tours and a few days off between matches, there was time aplenty during the Australian tour of England in 1934. Matches were widely spaced, so there was a plethora of rest days and that suited Mailey the artist to a tee.

He often set up his easel and paints on the sweeping tree-lined estate bordering the Royal House in Sandringham. One day King George V happened by during a morning stroll. He surprised Mailey,

Arthur Mailey: 'I bowled tripe, I wrote tripe and now I sell tripe.' (RONALD CARDWELL, THE CRICKET PUBLISHING COMPANY, WEST PENNANT HILLS, NSW)

whom he got to know well and grew to like through meeting him on two tours (1921 and 1926, when Arthur played) and in 1934 when he was covering the tour for an Australian newspaper. When the king suggested the sun in one of Mailey's paintings looked out of shape, the Australian replied: 'Your Majesty, since arriving in England I had almost forgotten what the sun looks like.' The great English cricket writer Neville Cardus called Mailey the 'most fascinating cricketer I have known and an artist in every part of his nature'.

Today Mailey is best remembered for his brilliant piece of writing about bowling to his hero Trumper. Mailey delivered the perfect wrong'un, which defeated the great man, who misread it for a leg break, the ball careering between bat and pad for the 'keeper to stump the batsman yards out of his ground: 'There was no triumph in me as I watched the receding figure. I felt like a boy who had killed a dove.'

Between 1921 and 1926 Mailey played 21 Test matches, taking 99 wickets at an average of 33.91. In 158 first-class matches he took

779 wickets at 24.09 with 61 bags of five wickets and 16 bags of 10 in a match.

Mailey's greatest bowling analysis was his 10/66 for Australia in the second innings against Gloucestershire at Cheltenham in 1921. That performance inspired the title of his 1958 autobiography: *10 for 66 and all that.*

One sentence from the book bears consideration: 'It is quite possible that powerful television corporations will buy up Test teams, lock, stock and barrel and "can" the match distribution throughout cricket-loving countries.' It's not that Mailey had a crystal ball to see what Kerry Packer's Channel Nine would do in the 1970s, but it is an indication of the man's extraordinary vision.

He wrote further:

At sixteen I was given the opportunity to become a glassblower. A galvanised iron shed in which a furnace melted glass to a light amber liquid was my next workroom. On a summer day the heat was intense. Even without the furnace the unprotected shed registered 110 degrees Fahrenheit in the shade. The floor was of roughly laid bricks which often burnt holes in my hobnailed blucher boots. This was hell all right, but it held at least three virtues. I became the youngest bottle blower in the state at a wage of £3 a week – half as much as an MP received in those days. It allowed me to buy decent clothes and pay the fee to join an art class. And, much more important perhaps, the continual spinning of the four-foot pipe which held the molten glass gave me fingers of great strength and toughness.

When bowling, my fingers never became calloused, worn or tired, and this, I feel, was responsible for the fact that I never met a bowler who could spin the ball more viciously than I, even if my direction or length were faulty. 'Chuck' Fleetwood-Smith might have been an exception.

Continual blowing expanded and strengthened my lungs and later enabled me to bowl hours without showing much sign of fatigue.

> Thinking back, I feel that greater use could have been made of my lung power when appealing, but as it was I seemed to get along on what was described by Neville Cardus as a 'somewhat apologetic whimper'.

When Mailey released this classic cricket book he had not played a Test for more than 30 years. Some friends were worried that the public may have forgotten him. He put them at ease by saying that all would be okay for 'the book will sell at least 7584 copies, because there are 7584 people in the English-speaking world who buy every book on cricket published'.

Mailey's attitude to spin bowling infuriated the likes of Bill O'Reilly and Clarrie Grimmett, both of whom hated giving away a single, let alone a flood of runs.

As a boy sitting on the SCG Hill, O'Reilly saw Mailey clean bowl Victorian batsman Les Keating with a ball that bounced twice before hitting the stumps. Later O'Reilly wrote:

> Mailey's philosophy allowed him to regard that delivery as a good ball – it got a wicket. Grimmett's reaction would have been contemptuous, as mine was, even though I was still in short pants and sitting on the Hill.

Grimmett watched 'in horror' as a Mailey full toss clean bowled Jack Hobbs at The Oval in 1926.

Even a Mailey full toss held its danger for the unwary. It descended from the skies with a sudden dip, for the ball had been spun viciously by those powerful fingers and supple wrist. Many a good player fell to the Mailey full toss.

Legend had it that his full toss was always a ball bowled on purpose. Two men – O'Reilly and Grimmett – reckoned that assertion to be pure poppycock.

A popular cricketer, Mailey was loved every bit for his humanity and humour as he was for his bowling. Mailey was one of those rare birds of that conservative age who well knew the value of publicity. And whenever he drew a cartoon he always had an image of himself in the corner, a picture that depicted him with a snub nose and a patch on his trousers. Mailey's sketch books and cartoons are now eagerly sought by cricket collectors.

When Victoria amassed 1107 runs in a Sheffield Shield match against NSW at the MCG in 1926, Mailey finished with figures of 4/362. To this day, no bowler has conceded more runs in a Sheffield Shield innings.

'Clearly my figures would have been better had that chap in the grey felt hat not dropped six sitters in the outer,' he quipped. 'I was just finding a length when the innings finished.'

He unexpectedly turned up at the London office of the Sydney *Daily Telegraph* in the northern summer of 1956 in the midst of a Test that was being played hundreds of miles north in Leeds.

'Arthur, why aren't you at the Test?' a work colleague enquired.

'Jack,' Mailey replied, speaking of the Australian team, 'They are so bad I can't bear to watch them, so I thought I'd buy you a champagne lunch instead.'

During the 1926 Australian tour of England, team manager Syd Smith rebuked Mailey for offering some of his spin bowling secrets to England leg spinner Ian Peebles.

'Well Syd, the answer is simple. Spin bowling is an art and art is international.'

One of his teammates once described Mailey's bowling as 'spin, flight and sheer fun'.

Impish, delightfully different and cheeky, perhaps Arthur Mailey knew more about the magic of spin than anyone of his time.

DON BLACKIE

The 'Rock'

Donald Dearness Blackie was a throwback to the old days of off spin and off cut by such exponents as Monty Noble, George Giffen and Bill Howell.

Born on 5 April 1882 in Bendigo, Blackie never dreamt that he might play Test cricket. He had long retired from first-class cricket before his doctor recommended he quit mowing lawns and digging weeds at weekends and return to playing for St Kilda and Victoria. His doctor must have been a spin bowling fan, for Blackie joined left-arm orthodox spinner Bert Ironmonger at St Kilda and they became Victoria's state team spin twins. Blackie made his first-class debut for Victoria in 1924–25 at the age of 42 and four years later, at the age of 46 years 253 days, Don Blackie was picked for the Australian Test team to play against England in the summer of 1928–29. He remains the oldest debutant to play in a Test for Australia. Blackie played three Test matches, taking 14 wickets: 4/148 off 59 overs on debut in Sydney; 6/94 and 1/75 in the Melbourne third Test and 1/57 and 2/70 in the Adelaide fourth Test. His 14-wicket haul placed him at the top of the Australian averages for the series, but he never played another game after Adelaide, continuing to play for Victoria until the end of the 1930–31 season. He toured New Zealand with an Australian side in 1927–28, taking 21 wickets at 19, including nine wickets in the two unofficial Tests with NZ. For Victoria his best match performance was against MCC at the MCG in 1929–30 with 5/82 and 7/25.

Blackie was nicknamed 'Rock' because of his habit of forgetting names. So instead of saying 'mate' or 'cove', he said 'G'day Rock.' The tables were turned, and everyone began calling him 'Rock'.

Wisden described Blackie as 'an off-break bowler of wiry physique who flighted the ball and allied swerve to spin and accuracy. He varied his pace skilfully from medium to slow medium.' The 'Rock' dismissed Don Bradman twice in the 1927–28 season (bowled for 5 and stumped for 7). In 47 first-class games Blackie took 211 wickets at 24.11, with 12 hauls of five wickets or more in an innings and twice he captured 10 or more wickets for a match.

Competing with Ironmonger, Mailey, and then Grimmett for a spot in the team, Rock was caught in a hard place.

BERT IRONMONGER

Nothing so dainty

Bert Ironmonger's fielding was awkward, clumsy, indeed hilarious. He was unbending and so consistently clumsy that he was dubbed 'Dainty' – but he did take one blinding catch. It was during the 1932–33 Bodyline series in the fifth Test at the SCG. Harold Larwood, the villain of the piece who became the main instrument of the Bodyline attack for England captain Douglas Jardine, was on 98, approaching what would have been his maiden Test century, when he struck a ball hard and low. Somehow Dainty Ironmonger hung on to the ball before it crashed into his right big toe. Larwood never did get a ton in Tests. Dainty's batting was similarly poor. Legend has it that Dainty's wife rang the dressing-room at the MCG during a Sheffield Shield match and was told her husband had just gone in to bat.

'Oh, that's okay … I'll wait,' she said.

But Ironmonger was a terrific spin bowler. A left-hand orthodox spinner, he was exceptionally accurate, possessed infinite patience and tended to wear the batsmen down.

On the flint-hard pitches that were produced in Australia between the wars, Ironmonger managed to tie down the finest batsmen England and Australia could produce; and when rain and sun did their thing on uncovered wickets, he was all but unplayable and made batsmen look foolish.

He suffered a horrific injury to his bowling hand while working in a timber mill in Ipswich, Queensland, before the Great War. While explaining to his foreman how an accident had occurred he lost half of his middle finger to a circular saw in the demonstration. That's clumsy.

He played his early cricket in Queensland, but was advised to move state if he wanted to play at the top level. Just before he left Queensland for Victoria in the summer of 1913–14, he played for Queensland against the star-studded NSW team. NSW hit 571 in its first innings and Ironmonger bowled 38 teasing overs, garnering the wickets of Victor Trumper, Herbie Collins, Tommy Andrews and Charles Kelleway for a return of 5/158.

In the 1914–15 season he had match figures of 5/91 for Victoria against NSW and in the return game 8/137; in two matches against South Australia he returned match figures of 13/181 and 6/139.

In the summer of 1920–21 Ironmonger turned up in Sydney to work on the docks at Sydney Harbour. In Sydney that summer he played 12 games for Balmain, taking 51 wickets at 12.80. When Hugh Trumble, by that time the Melbourne Cricket Club secretary, got wind of Ironmonger having gone to Sydney, he set about luring the cricketing nomad back to Melbourne. Trumble, the great off spinner before the Great War, was greatly impressed with Ironmonger's bowling and to get him to agree to move from Sydney he needed to arrange a job for him. Dainty was 42 by the time he moved back to Victoria in the summer of 1924–25. He didn't play a lot of state cricket but he was given a chance to play against Arthur Gilligan's visiting MCC team. In that match at the MCG he got a hat-trick. By the 1927–28 season he had become a permanent member of the Victorian team.

Dainty played his first Test in 1928, in the first Test against the touring Englishmen. At 45 years 237 days he was the second oldest player to make his Test debut in Australia. There was another debutant in the Australian side that day, a fresh 20-year-old by the name of Bradman, who made 18 and 1. Ironmonger took two wickets in each innings. Bradman was dropped for the second test; Ironmonger held his place in the team.

Two years later he had match figures of 11/79 against the West Indies in 1930–31. Learie Constantine, the West Indian all-rounder, found Bert Ironmonger the most difficult of all bowlers to fathom, and Clarrie Grimmett was among those bowlers.

In the 1932–33 Bodyline series against England Dainty took 15 wickets. In just 14 Test matches he took 74 wickets at 17.97. Imagine what he might have achieved had he settled down with Victoria as a young man.

The Ironmonger–Blackie partnership for the St Kilda Cricket Club in Melbourne was amazing. There they were, two old blokes spinning away from dawn to dust. As spinners they seemed ageless, timeless. When Ironmonger walked off the SCG at the end of the last innings of the Bodyline series, having taken the only two wickets to fall, he was 50 years and 327 days old. He died in his sleep aged 89 at his St Kilda home – where the Junction Oval grandstand still bears his name.

CLARRIE GRIMMETT

'My breath of life'

All Clarrie Grimmett's birthdays and Christmases came at once, for he was born on 25 December 1891, in New Zealand. Early in his life the family moved from the suburb of Caversham, Dunedin, in New Zealand's South Island to Wellington. And it was on the streets of Wellington and at the city's famous ground, Basin Reserve, that the young Grimmett honed his skill.

Next door to the Grimmetts' Roxburgh Street house lived the Harris family. George Harris, the eldest of the three Harris boys, was disabled, but he wasn't wheelchair bound. He moved about on crutches. An avid cricket fan, George Harris created scorecards that were to Clarrie 'works of art'. The Harris boys loved bowling leg breaks, and so too did Clarrie, although he was for some time the terror fast bowler among the junior cricket fraternity of Wellington. All the boys played cricket in the street; from the time they got home from school to the time their mothers called them to dinner it was cricket, cricket, cricket and spin, spin, spin. George Harris was 15, Charles 10 and Arthur eight. Clarrie was aged seven in the early summer of 1899. Each day when the gloom set in over Wellington, these cricket urchins scattered in all directions at the sudden appearance of Constable Thirsk. The rotund Thirsk was a gentle soul but his presence astride his trusty steed was always too much for the boys. They always ducked for cover. Constable Thirsk would smile, noting the arms and legs protruding at odd and ungainly angles from the roadside hedge.

Basin Reserve became a magnet for the boys. Most of the ground was in excellent order in those days, but a portion of the ground was neglected; it was as rough as a cow paddock. The cricket authorities allowed the local urchins to play on this area. Clarrie was entrusted to bring along a spade and smooth out the rough spots on their crude 'pitch'. From his early days bowling on this rough pitch Clarrie found that it was the combination of flight and breadth of turn that would defeat a batsman.

He was the smallest boy of the four but was determined to keep up with the Harris brothers, for they all possessed the ability to make their leg breaks curve in flight, turn and bounce. Clarrie discovered the harder he spun the ball the more acutely the ball would dip. It would also make a curious humming sound.

At Mount Cook Boys' School in Wellington, Clarrie was for a long time the 'gun' fast bowler. He loved bowling leg breaks with the Harris boys in the impromptu games at Basin Reserve, but he did not believe that spin was the go in 'real' matches for the school.

Mount Cook Boys' School nets became the place to learn the art of cricket. The school sports master, FA 'Dimp' Hempelmann, ruled those net sessions with an iron fist. The boys loved and admired him for his love of sport, but they also feared making an error in his presence.

It was the general practice for each bowler to finish every session by bowling six balls in succession. This was a test of character. The sports master knew the boys would be dead tired; he wanted to see which boys had the determination to finish the session bowling with all the energy they possessed.

One afternoon Clarrie was letting fly with the first couple of fast deliveries of his final six. But with just two balls to go, Clarrie was nearly spent, so he came in and bowled a beautifully flighted leg break. The ball curved in and gripped on the responsive turf, spinning prodigiously across the batsman to hit off stump. Hempelmann could hardly contain his glee.

'Another leg break, if you please, Mr Grimmett!'

Clarrie turned in another cracking leg break. Hempelmann pronounced: 'From now on, Mr Grimmett, you shall bowl leg breaks and only leg breaks. Yes, from this day forth young man it is leg breaks.'

In his next match, against Wairarapa School, his figures were 6/5 and 8/1. Hempelmann was right.

Later that summer Clarrie decided to skip school and go to the Basin Reserve. Monty Noble's Australian team was in town playing a Wellington XI and there was the chance that Victor Trumper would be batting.

Clarrie was, at 14, small and frail. There was no worry about having to have his Sunday best made to measure; there was always a suit for Grimmett straight off the hook. This day, the sunny Saturday of 17 March 1905, Clarrie dressed in his new blue suit.

Entrance money was not required, for the urchins of Wellington knew a better way to enter the ground – over the barbed wire that stretched along the top of the thick brick wall running the perimeter of the ground. In his haste to get over the wire Clarrie tore a huge hole in his trousers, and he knew he would cop 'old Harry' when his mother discovered the damage, but in years to come he always said it was worth it, for he got to see Trumper in full flight. As it turned out Trumper batted down the list so Clarrie had to wait for a few of the Australians to depart before his hero emerged. The great batsman of the Golden Age of cricket hit a masterly 171, with

20 fours and four sixes in his 269-run partnership with Clem Hill, which required just 117 minutes.

In 1914 Grimmett, now 23, played a few first-class matches for Wellington, including a match against an Australian XI, which included his hero, Trumper.

And while Clarrie didn't take a wicket he did bowl one over to Trumper, conceding two runs. During the lunch break on the first day of the match, the Australians indicated to the Wellington players that they would be happy to talk to them about technique and strategy. In those days Clarrie could bowl the wrong'un and the leg break with equal accuracy. However, he was interested to find out how Arthur Mailey, the great Australian legend of leg spin, bowled one.

> I asked him politely how he bowled the Bosey. Without saying a word, Mailey picked up the ball, ran leisurely into the empty net and delivered a nicely spun Bosey, which, upon pitching, turned appreciably from the off. This demonstration didn't convey much to me, so I asked Mailey if he didn't mind showing me again. Mailey didn't say a word. He ran in again, bowled another Bosey, then walked away.

Grimmett was not impressed with Mailey's performance. He needed to see at close hand and in slow motion how the ball left the hand. He needed a proper explanation. It steeled his resolve to one day play Test cricket and replace Mailey as the Test spinner – and that would come to pass.

Clarrie Grimmett dreamed of playing Test cricket, but New Zealand had not yet been granted Test match status. So in the late summer of 1914, as war descended over Europe, Clarrie sailed into Sydney from his native NZ seeking cricket fame.

The Great War prevented Australia's cricketers the chance to represent their respective states in first-class cricket, but grade cricket did continue for those not at the front.

Clarrie had won a medal for rifle shooting back in Wellington, but he didn't go to war. In all the writings of him and in my talks with Clarrie the subject of his not going to war never came up. I was interested only in his cricket, in particular his bowling.

Clarrie spent more than four years in Sydney, but the cricket selectors there could not see past Mailey, so Clarrie was often overlooked. Jack Saunders, an old Australian Test match left-arm medium pacer, coached in Auckland before moving to Melbourne – where he urged Clarrie to move to.

Clarrie did play, playing for South Melbourne and Prahran and the odd match for Victoria but never establishing a permanent spot in the side, despite getting bumper harvests of wickets in club cricket. As the years passed he thought the chances of his dream to play Test cricket might well be dashed. As he had in Wellington and in Sydney, Clarrie fashioned a full-sized cricket pitch in his backyard. There he bowled alone at the stumps for hours. He trained a little fox terrier named Joe to fetch the balls and Joe did his work admirably.

Every Sunday Clarrie's wife, Lizzy, set off to church, but Clarrie stuck religiously to bowling in the backyard. Cricketing mates often came by to say hello and sometimes have a hit. One of these mates was the then very young Bill Ponsford and the Victorian wicketkeeper Jack Ellis.

One Sunday Jack threw a ball into the empty net while the players were having a break and enjoying a cool drink. 'C'mon Joe, fetch the ball. C'mon get the ball.'

Joe was taking a nap under the big red gum at the end of the garden. It was a hot day and Joe showed not the slightest inclination to obey Jack's request. Jack called again and Joe condescended to open one eye. Joe then focused on his master, Clarrie, who was as eager as anyone else to see what Joe might do. The dog had never before been tested in this way. Jack threw another ball into the empty net, then another. Despite repeated calls by Jack for Joe to fetch the ball, the dog showed total disdain; now yawning and stretching under the shade of that big gum. Clarrie finished his drink, laughing. 'Here's how to do it,' he said.

The master spinner picked up a ball and walked back briskly to his mark. He skipped in to bowl and delivered. Joe opened one eye, then closed it. Clarrie then nominated the stump he intended hitting.

'Bosey to pitch off and hit leg; leg break to pitch leg and hit off …'

Immediately the eighth ball had been delivered. Joe sprang into action. He leapt from under the red gum and scampered to the empty net, grabbed a ball in his mouth and dashed back to place it on the ground at the top of Clarrie's mark. Within a minute or so all of the balls were at Clarrie's feet.

Young Ponsford, who went on to become the most prolific scorer, behind Bradman, in first-class cricket, said: 'Yer know, that dog, little Joe Grimmett, might be famous one day!'

The grade wickets continued to fall to Grimmett's wiles, but opportunities to play for Victoria were scarce. Then one day, out of the blue, he got an invitation for another first-class game.

He was selected for Victoria to play South Australia at Adelaide Oval. His selection came in the wake of two stalwarts – Jack Ryder and Jack Ellis – declaring themselves unavailable for the match. Already Clarrie was being wooed by the South Australians, especially the Adelaide Cricket Club and men such as the SA captain Vic Richardson and then SA selector Clem Hill. Clarrie took 1/12 and 8/86 and in the winter the Grimmett family – Clarrie, Lizzy and son Victor – set out for Adelaide. AG 'Johnnie' Moyes once described Adelaide as 'the haven for unwanted bowlers and the staging post to England'.

Grimmett was an immediate success for SA. At 32 years of age he could see that he must grab his opportunity. This was his last chance. The joy of Test selection came for Clarrie in the final Ashes Test the next season, the 1924–25 summer.

His first over in Test cricket was delivered to the great England left-hander Frank Woolley.

Clarrie once described to me that first exciting over.

I was thrilled at being given the ball but I was not really nervous because I have always had supreme confidence in my bowling and in my ability to maintain a length. The more important the match, the better I can concentrate. However, I felt a bit anxious because I knew I could put the ball where I wanted but I did not know what Woolley would do with it. Woolley hit my third ball, a stock leg break, to the cover boundary. It was then I decided to give him a high, slower leg break hoping to outwit him. I reckoned he might think it a Bosey and leave a gap between his front pad and bat. My plan worked. I sent down an ordinary leg break and he seemed to lose sight of it. Then came the death rattle of the stumps falling – the sweetest sound a bowler knows.

Herbie Collins was captaining Australia. Collins had been Clarrie's first captain for the Sydney club back in 1915, and he preferred Grimmett over Mailey. So Clarrie got first use of the ball. Collins's instincts were dead right: Grimmett took 5/45 and 6/37.

Clarrie's partnership with Bill O'Reilly really whetted the appetites of cricket followers. In 1934 they toured England together. There they were magnificent. O'Reilly wrote:

It was on that tour that we had all the verbal bouquets in the cricket world thrown at us as one of the greatest spin combinations Test cricket had seen. Bowling tightly and keeping the batsmen unremittingly on the defensive, we collected 53 (Grimmett 25, O'Reilly 28) of the 73 English wickets that fell that summer.

Each of us collected more than 100 wickets on tour and it would have needed a brave, or demented, Australian at that time to suggest that Grimmett's career was almost ended.

O'Reilly was not alone in his reckoning that he and Grimmett bowled in perfect harmony, each with a careful eye for the other.

> With Grum at the other end I knew full well that no batsman would be allowed the slightest respite. We were fortunate in that our styles supplemented each other. Grum loved to bowl into the wind, which gave him an opportunity to use wind resistance as an important adjunct to his schemes regarding direction. He had no illusions about the ball 'dropping' as we hear so often these days before its arrival at the batsman's proposed point of contact. To him that was balderdash. In fact, he always loved to hear people making up verbal explanations for the suspected trickery that had brought a batsman's downfall. If a batsman had thought the ball had dropped all well and good. Grimmett himself knew that it was simply change of pace that had made the batsman think that such an impossibility had happened.

O'Reilly was adamant that a spinning ball does not suddenly drop and that loop and dip is non-existent. It is a maverick position, one with which I totally disagree. The more over spin you put on a ball, the more acute the drop. A hard-spun leg break also curves in towards the right-hander; the more spin, the more the ball curves and the greater chance it has to curve late. Conversely an off spinner can make a ball curve away from the right-hander. It happens by spinning the ball hard; the greater the purchase on the ball, the more the ball curves. An off spinner needs a high arm and if the bowler operates with a high arm and spins hard, the ball curves away and drops. Grimmett himself always talked about bowling a dipping flight and bowling a trajectory to get the ball above the batsman's eye-line.

From 1924 to 1941 Grimmett wheeled down 28,467 balls for South Australia and he still heads the all-time wicket tally in the Sheffield Shield with 513 wickets at 25.29. That record is in no immediate danger – the closest of the current players is 230 wickets in arrears.

In 37 Tests he took 216 wickets at 24.21. In first-class cricket he bagged 1424 wickets at 22.58 with a career-best innings effort of 10/37 against Yorkshire in 1930.

In 248 first-class matches Clarrie Grimmett took bags of five wickets or more in a single innings 127 times. Don Bradman hit 117 centuries in 234 matches. If you equate a five-wicket haul with a century, Grimmett's bowling record is better than Bradman's batting record.

In March 1991 Sir Donald Bradman wrote this to me about Clarrie Grimmett:

> I always classified Clarrie Grimmett as the best of the genuine slow leg spinners, (I exclude Bill O'Reilly because he was not really a slow leggie) and what made him the best, in my opinion, was his accuracy. Arthur Mailey spun the ball more – so did Fleetwood-Smith and both of them bowled a better wrong'un but they also bowled many loose balls. I think Mailey's wrong'un was the hardest of all to pick.
>
> Clarrie's wrong'un was in fact easy to see. He telegraphed it and he bowled very few of them. His stock-in-trade was the leg spinner with just enough turn on it, plus a really good top-spin delivery and a good flipper (which he cultivated late in life). I saw Clarrie in one match take the ball after some light rain when the ball was greasy and hard to hold yet he reeled off five maidens without a loose ball. His control was remarkable.

The Don noted that Bill O'Reilly was not a slow leg spinner. Bradman always maintained that O'Reilly was the best bowler of them all.

Most importantly of all, Grimmett invented the flipper, which Shane Warne at the height of his brilliant career bowled so well.

Like Grimmett, Warne did not have a great wrong'un, but he possessed a terrific stock leg break and a stunning top-spinner.

Grimmett always wore a scarlet woollen vest under his cricket shirt and, while he was often called 'Grum', 'The Old Fox' and 'The Miser', his most commonly used nickname was 'Scarlet'.

Grimmett dismissed Bradman 10 times in his career, including at the Grimmett–Richardson Testimonial match at the Adelaide Oval in November 1937.

Late on the Friday Vic Richardson said: 'Scarlet we need a wicket badly, but we also want Bradman to stay for the bumper crowd tomorrow.'

Bradman had earlier implied that Grimmett had lost his ability to turn his leg break.

Just before stumps, Grimmett spun a leg break prodigiously to defeat the master:

Bradman, bowled Grimmett, 17.

Clarrie gave a triumphant jig and Richardson yelled: 'Scarlet, you bloody fool. You've just cost us a thousand quid!'

A few years earlier, during the 1930 Australian tour of England both Grimmett and Bradman were starring in the Test and county matches. Bradman of course received letters in their hundreds; Clarrie received this charming letter from an Irish schoolgirl, Ida Burke. It reads in part:

You remind me of Puck or Punch for you are rather tiny, aren't you? Or some sort of Irish Leprechaun, that live at the bottom of Lake Killarney – dear little folk they are, but all alive and up to mischief.

You know you would make a cute little Irishman. This letter is to wish you luck with the ball. I would like to read of you doing something really startling. Can't I then read of Grimmett breaking all records – Bradman becomes boring – even all the school girls know of Don Bradman, who does seem a bit of a darlin' but – I began this because I had nothing to do. I will finish now for I have nothing to say. Yours with best wishes, Ida Burke.

The cricketing heroes were rarely seen other than at the ground or the odd snapshot in the newspapers. Radio was of the crackling kind, spasmodic. Television had not yet invaded our lounge rooms, so writing letters – real letters, hand written and in a hand that was totally legible – was the natural way of communicating with them. The newspapers meanwhile, especially in England, were full of excellent cricket writing – and Neville Cardus, the Shakespeare of the game's writers, was king.

From 1940 until the end of 1945 Cardus lived in Sydney. One day in 1940 Clarrie bumped into the writer in a Sydney street.

Cardus was lamenting the loss of Europe and Britain's fine architecture and art treasures, whereupon Clarrie quipped: 'Yes, Neville, I am very sad about it. You see I've developed this new ball and I won't be able to test it in top company. Blast the war!'

An impish character he was, attracting attention wherever he went not because of his brashness but because he was precisely the opposite, quiet and mysterious. Clarence Victor Grimmett loved the game of cricket, and spin bowling was his greatest love of all. He used to say spin bowling was 'my breath of life'.

LESLIE FLEETWOOD-SMITH

Our greatest Chinaman bowler

They say all spinners need a break. Leslie O'Brien 'Chuck' Fleetwood-Smith got one: he broke his right arm in a fall from a tree as a teenager, and went from being a right-arm leg spinner to a left-arm wrist spinner.

The left-arm wrist spinner is universally known as a 'Chinaman' bowler and Fleetwood-Smith was Australia's most famous exponent of the art.

The legend of the Chinaman began back in 1933 during the Old Trafford Test match. West Indian left-arm orthodox spinner Ellis 'Puss' Achong suddenly bowled a wrist spinner. Instead of spinning the ball slightly away from the batsman, the ball dipped suddenly and spun back in to the right-hander to have him stumped. England batsman Walter Robins was so shocked to be dismissed in this way he said on his return to the pavilion, 'fancy being done by a Chinaman'.

Fleetwood-Smith was educated at Melbourne's exclusive private school Xavier College, which has produced many a brilliant cricketer and Australian Rules footballer. When Fleetwood-Smith first began bowling his left-handed 'twirlies', his mates at school used to call them 'corkscrew' deliveries. He spun the ball so hard it hummed and when he got it right he could beat the best batsmen in the world.

Fleetwood-Smith was broad-shouldered and solidly built. He possessed strong wrists and fingers, developed by squeezing a squash ball. A complex character, he loved making bird calls on the field, or whistling a popular tune as he approached the wicket to bowl. He was expert in imitating the whipbird, making magpie calls and, when the mood struck him, producing unplayable deliveries. Sometimes during a tense moment in a big match, he would suddenly cry, 'C'mon, Port Melbourne!' – an inexplicable reference to an Australian Rules football team.

The Adelaide Test was the defining match of the 1936–37 Ashes summer. Wally Hammond's wicket was the key to Australia's chances of a win.

Chasing 391, England was well set as the fifth day commenced, at 3/148, with the genius Hammond at the crease, resuming his inning on 39. Captain Bradman handed the ball to Chuck, whom he dubbed 'this wayward genius' and told him the match – and the Ashes – depended upon him. Bradman later wrote that Fleetwood-Smith bowled 'a glorious sinuous ball which swerved away from the bat but then viciously spun back between bat and pad as the flight drew Hammond forward'. Bill O'Reilly, who was on the field that day, agreed, saying it was the 'finest ball I have ever seen delivered in big cricket.' It was the ball of the century – until Shane Warne came along.

Hammond was out clean bowled and Australia won the match by 148 runs. 'If ever the result of a Test match can be said to have been decided by a single ball, this was the occasion,' Bradman wrote. And his analysis was correct: a win in the next match meant Australia won the series 3–2.

That Adelaide match was Fleetwood-Smith's best in Test cricket. He took 4/129 and 6/110, his 10-wicket haul ensuring the Australian victory.

His last Test was the fifth Test at The Oval in 1938. England batted first and scored 903 for the loss of seven wickets before a declaration was made, easing Australia's agony.

O'Reilly and Fleetwood-Smith did the bulk of the bowling. O'Reilly bowled 85 overs and finished with 3/187; Fleetwood-Smith spun down 87 overs to take 1/298. No bowler has ever conceded more Test runs in one innings. His one wicket was the great Hammond, whom he dismissed six times in their 15 meetings. For England Len Hutton made 364, beating the world record of 334 set by Don Bradman at Leeds in 1930. Bradman badly injured his ankle when bowling and could not bat in either of the Australian innings. Nor could Jack Fingleton, who was also injured and England won the match by a massive innings and 579 runs.

This was the nation's greatest Test match defeat. O'Reilly recalled fondly that late on the second day as England was grinding his team into The Oval's dust, Fleetwood-Smith called out to him from the boundary. 'My left-handed spin partner let out an extraordinary roar: "Hey 'Tiger' (O'Reilly) I actually got my off-break to turn!"'

They called Fleetwood-Smith 'Chuck' throughout his first-class career, which produced 597 wickets at 22.64. Despite touring England twice (1934 and 1938) and South Africa in 1935–36, he played just 10 Tests taking 42 wickets at 37.38. However, he was better, much better than his figures reflect.

O'Reilly said:

He was the best left-handed spinner of his day and if his temperament had allowed him to concentrate fully on developing his magnificent talents he would have been rated as the greatest spinner of all time.

Bradman said that at his best he

> could deceive anybody as to which way the ball would turn and his great
> spin and nip off the pitch were most disconcerting. This necessarily
> brought inaccuracy in its train and many a time he became the despair
> of his captain because of his loss of control.' Unfortunately for him he
> played at a time when the spin-twins Grimmett and O'Reilly reigned
> supreme. There was rarely room for a third spinner in the side.

Chuck married in 1935 and divorced in 1946, after his return
from service in the AIF. He was a big, handsome man, debonair
with a neat moustache and the look of Clark Gable about him: very
popular, they said, with the ladies. But after his cricket he fell on
hard times. The demon drink got him and he became best known
to the metho drinkers and the homeless who gathered in the parks
near the MCG, the site of some of his best sporting successes.

In April 1969 he appeared in the Melbourne City Court on a
charge of vagrancy.

He told reporters outside the courthouse that all he wanted was
'a bed, a meal and a few beers'. Old mates and cricketers helped him
where they could and when he allowed them to help.

Ian Chappell knew the sad story of Chuck's final days. Chappelli's
grandfather Vic Richardson was Chuck's Australian captain on the
tour of South Africa in 1935–36 .

> Vic didn't mention Chuck to me, but Tiger (O'Reilly) told me he could
> spin the ball a mile and bowl the odd unplayable ball. Tiger didn't think
> Chuck's bird calls from mid-on endeared him to Bradman.

During a Boxing Day Test in Melbourne Chappell and Bob
'Fergie' Massie, formerly a swing bowler for WA and Australia,
were taken by legendary Victorian cricketer, administrator and

commentator Bill Jacobs to the spot where Chuck used to sleep rough on the banks of the Yarra River.

'It was round Boxing Day in Melbourne and it was bloody freezing,' Chappelli recalls.

Three years after that court appearance Fleetwood-Smith left us, aged 62.

Chuck Fleetwood-Smith will always be remembered as Test cricket's 'wayward genius', who also happened to be Australia's greatest left-arm wrist spinner; the nation's best Chinaman bowler.

BILL O'REILLY

The Tiger

Bill O'Reilly was the greatest Australian spinner of the 1930s. A right-arm leg spinner, O'Reilly was called 'The Tiger', for he was aggressive, ferocious in his approach and his execution. It was certainly not because he was lithe and athletic like a tiger; O'Reilly's approach to the wicket was more akin to a bull in a china shop: gangly, all arms and legs. He spun his variety of leg breaks and wrong'uns with a high arm action at medium pace, a lot quicker through the air than most leg spinners. When got his dander up, which was often, O'Reilly's red hair stood out like an Irish revolt.

Bill Brown, the Queensland and Australia opening batsman of the era, saw a lot of the Tiger, playing against him in Sheffield Shield cricket and with him in Tests. They were teammates on the 1934 and 1938 Test tours of England. He said of O'Reilly:

> He operated at a slow medium pace, yet he managed to get the ball to bounce. Indeed his googly used to bounce like a tennis ball and was spun

so hard it seemed to crawl up the face of the bat and present one of his short-leg fieldsmen with a dolly of a catch.

At various stages the Tiger's 'suicide squad' of short-leg fieldsmen were Jack Fingleton, Len Darling, Bill Brown and Sid Barnes. The Tiger aimed at the line of the leg stump to the right-handers, because if they missed the ball he wanted it to hit off stump. There were no half measures about O'Reilly. His appeals for lbw were always loud and demanding. When an appeal was dismissed the Tiger walked back to his mark hurt by the rebuff but clearly even more determined to win the day. O'Reilly loved the challenge of bowling to Don Bradman, one whom he particularly liked to slay.

O'Reilly's name is inextricably linked with Bradman's, and their early battles are the stuff of legend.

At the height of the 1925–26 summer, 19-year-old O'Reilly first pitted his skill against the 16-year-old Bradman. I had vaguely heard about this famous encounter, O'Reilly representing Wingello and Bradman playing at home for Bowral, at what is now the Bradman Oval.

It was some time in the 1980s when Bill and I caught up after watching a Test in Brisbane, Bill having completed his piece for *The Sydney Morning Herald* and me away from the ABC microphone for the day.

'Son, I know a good spot up the road from where I am staying near the Gabba. It's called the Pineapple Hotel. We used to frequent the place when we played up here in the 1930s. A cold beer would do us a treat,' Bill enthused.

Over a few coldies Bill delivered a lengthy discourse about the first time he bowled to Bradman.

I was working for Sydney Teachers' College and had a few days off during the holidays. I told fellow student Len Kelsey that I would be playing a few games for Wingello in the Southern Tablelands.

'I must warn you Bill, of a youngster named Don Bradman; knew him at Bowral High. Brilliant bat,' Kelsey said. 'He has been getting runs at will and he will test the best he comes up against.'

Bill said he was not perturbed about this pint-sized youngster from Bowral.

Bill boarded a train at Sydney's Central Station, bound for Goulburn. That Saturday in December 1925 turned out hot, not a cloud in the sky – perfect for a game of cricket. The train came to a halt at Bowral and over the sound of hissing steam O'Reilly heard his name being called by the stationmaster.

'Get your bag, O'Reilly, and get off the train!'

The stationmaster explained: 'We're all down here to play Bowral this afternoon. And you're getting the new ball. All is arranged. Your mum has packed your cricket clothes and you'll be driven straight from the station to the ground.'

Bill recalled clambering onto the back of a 1918 vintage T-model Ford truck, where those already seated on facing wooden benches briefed him fully on the growing reputation of Don Bradman. Bill then realised that he was there specifically to quell the brilliance of the youngster.

'When we arrived at the ground we all dressed under the shade of two massive gum trees near the grandstand,' Bill smiled.

Bowral won the toss and batted. Midway through the third over O'Reilly bowled one of the openers and all eyes turned to the incoming batsman.

'When I saw this diminutive figure struggling to reach the wicket in pads clearly too big for him I couldn't help but break into a grin.

'"He's mine," I thought.'

After a few balls, Bill, the trainee school teacher, realised he had encountered his first problem child.

The Wingello captain was the rotund Selby Jeffrey, a veteran of the Gallipoli campaign, and the man responsible for having O'Reilly play in the match.

'Selby always fielded at first slip,' Bill said.

He wore a sparkling white shirt, immaculate duck trousers and a black waistcoat, worn unbuttoned, over his shirt. The waistcoat was an essential part of his dress, for it held his bent-stemmed Captain Peterson pipe and tobacco pouch which fitted snugly into one pocket, with the tin box of matches and a penknife for cutting a plug of tobacco in the bottom pocket.

Selby had to field at slip for as soon as he got out of the slowest of canters his smoking paraphernalia would have been scattered in all directions.

Much to O'Reilly's disgust Bradman was dropped twice before he scored 30. Once he had Bradman edge a ball that he'd got to turn and bounce alarmingly.

'The ball sailed gently to Selby at first slip at waist level and struck him in the solar plexus at the precise moment both Selby's hands were otherwise occupied,' Bill laughed. 'Our captain was lighting his pipe!'

Another drop and a drat in the thirties, then Bradman cut loose, thrashing the Wingello attack unmercifully to end the day at 234 not out.

Hostilities were to resume the following Saturday.

During the week O'Reilly tossed up in his mind about quitting cricket and concentrating on a tennis career or getting more serious about running for the Botany Harriers Athletics Club. His pride dented, O'Reilly bowled all week at the family home front gate. He was keen to make amends against this whippersnapper of a whiz kid.

News of Bradman's batting spread like wildfire in the tablelands and a big crowd was expected the following Saturday. In my poem *The Battle of Bowral*, I explain what happened:

Townsfolk in droves arrived just in time
To see the young warriors; a battle sublime.
They saw young O'Reilly bowl that first spinning ball
Young Don tapped his bat, a wicket must fall.
Arms wheeling away in hot noon sun,
O'Reilly moved in, his homework was done.
Don eyed with suspicion that O'Reilly first ball,
His footwork so keen, his score so tall.
The ball fairly buzzed, an ace and a trump,
It pitched leg perfect and hit the off stump!

William Joseph O'Reilly was born in the opal-mining town of White Cliffs, NSW, on Wednesday 20 December 1905. Bill was the fourth of seven children to Ernest Peter O'Reilly and Mina O'Reilly (née Welsh). O'Reilly was, like Bradman, a self-taught cricketer. Bill learned to play the game with his brothers in the backyard. They played with a crudely hewn gum-wood bat and a piece of banksia root chiselled down in the shape of a ball. At school Bill embraced the English language and one day in 1914 he met one of his heroes – who was no cricketer.

There stood eight-year-old Bill O'Reilly under a gas lamp in the misty rain at a spot near where the entrance to Sydney's Luna Park now stands.

There were three men approaching me as they emerged from the floodlit bar to hail me in the mist. I realised that my two jovial relatives were accompanied by a person who looked familiar to me but one whom I could not readily name. It was Henry Lawson, whose likeness I had seen so regularly in copies of the *Bulletin*.

That imposing red-covered magazine was my father's Bible. Meeting Henry Lawson made my ego jump higher than the flickering gas lamp which was shining high over my head.

'Mr Lawson, this is my son, Bill, who knows quite a lot about you and your poetry. Bill, I want you to meet my friend, Henry. You will be very proud when you are an old man that you've had this bit of good luck tonight.'

At the bar of the Pineapple Hotel, Bill ordered another cold one and turned to his great partnership with Clarrie Grimmett.

He first set eyes on Grimmett in 1919 when he saw the little leg spinner, by then domiciled in Melbourne, play in Goulburn.

Clarrie was in the Victorian team, which had played a match against NSW in Sydney and stopped in Goulburn to play the local side before the team's return to Victoria. Bill noted that the opening batsman's name on the scoreboard was spelt Grummett. From that day forth Clarrie became 'Grum' to Bill.

Clarrie Grimmett was the bowler I admired the most. I saw him perform in the fifth Test against England at the SCG in 1924. From that spectacular entry he made to Test cricket he became my personal model. His attitude towards dismissing batting opposition batsmen was inspiring to watch. He embraced his job in a dedicated manner which surely would have suggested to trade union officials that the boss had him working on a piecework incentive system, and that he was therefore a man to be watched carefully.

After he retired Bill wrote a regular cricket column for *The Sydney Morning Herald*. He developed his craft swiftly until finally he became a superb wordsmith, penning his daily comments by way of a lovely copperplate hand on an old dog-eared lined exercise book.

As time flew by workers began filing into the Pineapple Hotel, but we stayed put, lounging in facing wicker chairs. Another round and another story to whet the appetite of any cricket historian. This one was to transport me back to the very cradle of cricket in Australia.

Bill was wheeling away in the SCG nets late in the summer of the 1926–27 season when Arthur Mailey, who not long before had played his last Test, sidled up to him and suggested he change his grip.

'Thank you for your advice Mr Mailey,' the 20-year-old O'Reilly said respectfully, 'but I will stick with this grip. It has served me well since I was a youngster.'

Mailey had just walked away when Bill heard a voice from behind the net. 'They tried to change me too yer know, son, but I stuck to my guns and like you I politely, but firmly, told them that my grip is my grip. It doesn't need change. Good on you, son, well done.'

The voice from behind the net belonged to CTB Turner, the man they called 'the Terror'.

So the young Tiger came face to face with old CTB Turner, the prolific spinner of the 1880s. Advice passed from the old spinner to the young man. And in turn passed to me over a beer at the Pineapple.

Bill swallowed down another ale and said,

I must tell you this one. Grum (Grimmett) and I toured England just once together in 1934. One night after play at Lord's we were invited to the Pall Mall quarters of the famous writer, Sir James Barrie. Sir James was one to regale his guests with stories from the time they stepped through his front door.

Accompanying O'Reilly and Grimmett was Mailey, who was covering the tour for a newspaper group, and teammate Stan McCabe.

'I have formed a cricket team,' Sir James began.

I was the slowest bowler, in fact, I still am the slowest bowler, that ever bowled the right arm over. So slow indeed that after delivery I realised that something was wrong with the trajectory, I could retrieve it and set it properly on its course. One day, when bowling against the opposition's top batsman, I sent down a curly one and in letting it go, I cried, 'My God. He's out!'

So I sat down and watched the ball take its course. And as sure as I stand here now, it went up, evaded the bat and leaned against the off stump, just enough for one bail to fall.

Bill roared laughing and blurted, 'No wonder James Barrie wrote *Peter Pan*!'

I have spoken with many great batsmen who played with and against O'Reilly and they are all at one when speaking of his unique qualities as a spinner. Men such as Australia's Bill Brown, Don Bradman, Vic Richardson and Jack Fingleton, and England's Len Hutton, Denis Compton and Wally Hammond all agreed that he was truly great, perhaps the greatest spinner of them all.

Don Bradman was never in any doubt.

In a letter to me in the late 1980s, Sir Donald penned these words:

Of all the bowlers I played with and against, I rate Bill O'Reilly number one. In my opinion the hardest ball to play is the one which turns from leg to off and this was Bill's stock delivery. He persistently bowled at the right-hander's leg stump and, when perfectly pitched, that ball would

Bill O'Reilly, the bowler Don Bradman rates as the 'best ever'. (ASHLEY MALLETT COLLECTION)

take the off bail. There is precious little answer to such a delivery – the batsman usually gets an outside edge or the ball clips the off-stump.

Bill also bowled a magnificent Bosey which was hard to pick and which he aimed at middle and leg stumps. It was fractionally slower than his leg break and usually dropped a little in flight and 'sat up' to entice a catch to one of his two short-leg fieldsmen.

These two deliveries, combined with great accuracy and unrelenting hostility were enough to test the greatest of batsmen – particularly as his leg break was bowled at medium pace, quicker than the normal run of slow bowlers, thereby making it extremely difficult for a batsman to use his feet as a counter measure. Bill will always remain, in my book, the greatest of all.

In his 27 Tests Bill O'Reilly took 144 wickets at 22.59 apiece. Against England in 19 Tests he took 102 wickets at 25.36 each.

In all first-class matches O'Reilly took 774 wickets at 16.6 runs apiece. For NSW in 33 Sheffield Shield games O'Reilly took 203 wickets at 17.10 each. He skittled hundreds of batsmen for his beloved St George in Sydney grade cricket and was among the first inductees into the Australian Cricket Hall of Fame.

AFTER THE WAR

By 1946 Clarrie Grimmett had retired from first-class cricket. His spin twin Bill O'Reilly played the one-off Test match against New Zealand late in the summer of 1945–46 and then promptly slung his cricket boots out of the window at Basin Reserve, Wellington, and announced his career was over. This left a slew of good spinners all vying for a Test place.

Bruce Dooland, the SA leg spinner, Colin McCool, the Queensland slow leggie, Victoria's Doug Ring, and George Tribe, the Victorian Chinaman spinner, were all in the mix, but among the wrist spinners Dooland was the standout. Cec Pepper was probably the best of the bunch, but he was ruled out after his very public on-field tiff with Don Bradman at Adelaide Oval in 1946. The only finger spinner in contention was Victorian off spinner Ian Johnson. Johnson became a certain selection for the England tour in 1948, mainly because of the perception that finger spinners do better on the soft English pitches than leg spinners. Didn't anyone tell the selectors about O'Reilly and Grimmett? They did alright in England.

Dooland was unlucky, as was McCool, who played just 14 Tests and toured England in 1948 without playing a big match. McCool made his biggest impression in the UK, despite his lack of Tests there.

There were other spinners about, such as South Australia's Jack Wilson, who toured England in 1956 and had a day out against Somerset. Then there were the likes of Western Australia's

Chinaman specialist Tom O'Dwyer and leg spinner Tony Zimbulis. However, until the summer of 1947–48 WA was not in the Sheffield Shield competition and even then the state played just four matches to the other teams' eight. WA was given the right to double its points tally and in that first summer it won the Sheffield Shield.

BRUCE DOOLAND

A brilliant Test career swept aside

As leg spinners go Bruce Dooland was one of the very best, but circumstances conspired against him putting together a Test career. Dooland's early career was blocked by short-sighted officialdom. As a young bank officer he was first selected for South Australia in the summer of 1940–41, aged just 17. However, the bank manager would not allow him time off to play cricket. Then came the rather weightier matter of WWII. Dooland left the bank and served with distinction as a commando in the Pacific theatre of the war. Immediately after the war he was unfortunate to miss the 1948 Invincibles tour.

He played for South Australia and won three Test caps – two against England in 1946–47 and one against India in 1947–48. Dooland's three Test matches realised just nine wickets at the high cost of 46 runs apiece. He averaged just 19 with the bat, so his international cricket hardly turned a hair.

Colin McCool and Doug Ring beat him for a place in Bradman's Invincibles team bound for England in 1948, so Dooland did as others such as Cec Pepper and George Tribe had done: he set his sights on a professional career in England. As Bradman's men stormed through cricket-hungry England in the first Ashes series there since the war, Dooland batted and bowled with great skill to win the hearts of all East Lancashire supporters. He played four seasons with East Lancashire, helping the team win both the League Cup and the Worsley knock-out cup. During those years of consistent success Dooland took 361 wickets at 10 runs apiece and hit 2688 runs at an average of 38.

His great all-round skills attracted the Nottinghamshire County Cricket Club to engage his services and he made his county debut in May 1953 – the year Lindsay Hassett's Australian team toured England. In his first match for Notts against Kent at Trent Bridge, Dooland conceded 97 runs without taking a wicket. But he soon slipped into top gear, destroying Surrey, the champion county, at The Oval, with a match haul of 9/119. From there it was plain sailing in his first season, and he was unlucky to miss the double of 1000 runs and 100 wickets by a mere 30 runs. In five years with Notts Dooland took 748 wickets and scored 4492 runs. He twice achieved the 100/1000 double. He did well, but his decision to leave Australia and play in England almost certainly nipped a potentially brilliant Test career in the bud.

In 1953 and again the following year he was selected to play in the annual Players versus Gentlemen match at Lord's. The Players were professionals and the Gentlemen were the well-shod amateurs. When taking the field the Players entered the arena from a different gate than the Gentlemen. They also had separate change rooms in the pavilion. This was a throwback to the class system enshrined in the Victorian era: a real eye-opener for a young Australian making his way in the game.

Dooland was selected to represent the Commonwealth side that toured India in 1950–51, where he took seven wickets in five unofficial Tests.

He had played four seasons for South Australia, during which he took a hat-trick against Victoria, before he moved to England, and after his golden summers with Notts came to an end Dooland returned to Adelaide to turn out once more for SA in 1957–58. That summer I was in Adelaide playing for Western Australia in what is now known as the Under-17s National Championships. Slightly odd, that, given most of us were just 12 or 13 years of age. One morning I entered the John Martin's department store and headed for the downstairs eatery. Accompanied by a couple of my teammates, probably Des Philby (who in later years became a terrific baseball pitcher) and Graham Marsh (Rod Marsh's brother, later to become a famous golfer). We sat together and ordered. I suddenly caught sight of a familiar face sitting alone at a table reading a newspaper. The man was tall, very tanned, with distinctive curly hair and I could see he had notably long fingers, a brilliant asset for any spin bowler.

'That's the leg spinner Bruce Dooland,' I blurted.

'Rubbish. No way he'd be here,' one of my teammates laughed.

I walked over, introduced myself and Mr Dooland graciously gave of his time talking to us about the game of cricket, and how good it had been to him.

'If you ever get to England to play cricket, remember the wickets are more conducive to spin, but you still must beat the batsman in the air,' he said.

Our team was invited to lunch at the Adelaide Oval that summer. I managed to catch a glimpse of Sir Donald Bradman, and also got to see Dooland bowl. As I recall, the Victoria batsman Jack Potter – who we will see has a vital role to play in the history of Australian spin bowling – played some lovely drives in scoring a classic century. Dooland doesn't get the recognition he deserves because none of his great moments came in Test matches. Figures and statistics never tell the full story of a player, even when they are in the Bradman or Warne bracket.

Dooland was tall and athletic. He approached the wicket with purpose; a strong action with a high arm. Years later when I laid eyes on Anil Kumble, the Indian leg spinner, his action reminded me of Dooland's. There was a certain grace of movement to Dooland. His action was repeatable, consistent, so too his length and direction. He could give the ball a big rip, but, rather like Kumble, control was his hallmark.

He could bowl the top-spinner and wrong'un, but one of his best variations was the flipper, a delivery handed to him and Cec Pepper by its inventor, Clarrie Grimmett. Dooland passed on the magic of the flipper to a young Richie Benaud. And Shane Warne learnt about it when he was at the Australian Cricket Academy. Part-time spinner Jack Potter showed him the delivery and Warne caught on fast and made the flipper his own.

An outstanding baseballer with a bullet-like throw from the boundary, Dooland was one of many cricketers who played the game in the winter months. He was a pitcher playing for the West Torrens Baseball club, SA and then Australia. Despite his brilliant throwing arm from long distance, he found himself in the main fielding in a short catching position. A number of Australia's best cricketers had the distinction of playing Test cricket and representing Australia in baseball. They include Ian Chappell, Colin Guest, Neil Harvey, Norm O'Neill and Vic Richardson.

Bruce Dooland possessed a huge dollop of the magic of spin until well into his 40s, for it was then he turned out for an Adelaide journalists' annual clash with a local Catholic college and took a hat-trick, with a leg break, a top-spinner, then a flipper – why, it was like knocking bottles off a wall. Married, with one son, Bruce was just 56 when he died suddenly at his Bedford Park, Adelaide, home in September 1980.

JACK IVERSON

A cricketing phenomenon

As the rain pelted down relentlessly on the roof of a leaky tent in the jungles of New Guinea during the height of WWII, an Australian soldier messed about with a ping-pong ball. Holding the ball between thumb and middle finger, he found that depending on which side of the ball he applied his middle finger to, it dipped and spun differently. When he flicked the right side of the ball and bowled, the ball swerved late and dramatically to the left, then upon landing it spun in like a big off-break. After hours of testing his skill he decided to try his method out on his mates sharing the tent. They would protect the stumps – a jerry can – with a wooden ruler. Jack found he could deliver an off-break, a leg break and a top-spinner all with the same flicking method – most importantly, without any obvious change in how he released the ball. Despite the rain, the heat, the insects and dodging the bullets and grenades that came courtesy of the Japanese Imperial Army, Iverson utilised every possible waking moment to perfect his new skill. He couldn't wait to have a crack with a real cricket ball and try his luck in Melbourne grade cricket.

Once back in Australia at war's end, the demobbed Iverson decided to play sub-district cricket in Melbourne. He announced to his wife: 'I plan to prove that my bent finger flicking of a cricket ball will take me to the very top of the game.'

He immediately joined Brighton Thirds, playing his first game at the age of 31 in 1946. By the 1946–47 season he was in the firsts and was catapulted into the Victorian state side, after moving from Brighton to play for the Melbourne Cricket Club in 1948–49. He was chosen for Victoria in the 1949–50 season. In his state debut he snared 6/47 against Western Australia, followed by 7/77 against South Australia. At season's end Iverson was rewarded with a tour of New Zealand with an Australian XI. In all matches there he took 75 wickets at seven runs apiece.

They called him 'Big Jake', a tall, gangling fellow with an ungainly gait. His batting was hopeless and in the field he was as clumsy as a newborn giraffe. Usually sent to mid-on, the perennial spot for hopeless fieldsmen, when the ball approached 'Big Jake' never fielded it with his hands. He usually stopped it with his boot and kicked it back to the bowler. The fast men didn't like his method, for it scuffed the shine off the ball, thus reducing their ability to swing the ball late. However, with Big Jake it was all about his extraordinary bowling. The Australian selectors believed Iverson might just be the man to pick in the Test team to play Freddie Brown's 1950–51 England team. He was duly picked and his bowling was sensational. Batsmen of the calibre of Len Hutton, Denis Compton, Cyril Washbrook and Reg Simpson were perplexed by Iverson's spin and steep bounce. In the Test series Iverson took 21 wickets at an average of 14.57. He trod on a ball in the Adelaide Test; hobbled through the fifth match, he never played big cricket again. He is also in the unusual position of having a batting average of 0.75.

Big Jake proved that all things are possible in the game of cricket for those who 'invent' new and exciting methods. He was a cricket phenomenon. He sauntered out of the game to resume work with the family real estate business.

Big Jake will long be remembered for that one golden summer of 1950–51.

IAN JOHNSON

He bowled with no socks

Ian William Johnson was born in the sports-mad city of Melbourne on 8 December 1918. Ian was the elder son of North Melbourne wine-and-spirit merchant William Johnson, a slow bowler of some repute, who became a Test selector. The South Melbourne Cricket Club chose Johnson to play A grade when he was just 16, then attending Wesley College, as an off spinner, good slips fieldsman and gritty batsman. His father wasn't worried about being accused of favouritism, for he had no compunction in picking his son for Victoria when Ian was barely 17. Johnson was the slowest of slow bowlers to grace the cricket fields of Australian first-class cricket in an era when most of the spinners tended to push the ball through hurriedly. But Johnson was tight and astute. He changed his pace cleverly and the batsmen who reckoned they could rush down the track and get Johnson's deliveries on the full were usually in for a big surprise.

Flight was the key to his bowling and he had the ability to get his stock off-break to dip and duck away from the right-handed batsman late.

As war menaced over Europe, Johnson joined the Royal Australian Air Force (RAAF), receiving his wings at the age of 24. He flew in a Beaufighter squadron in the south-west Pacific. During Johnson's war he spent many a day in a tent in the jungle. That took its toll on his feet, for when his socks got wet the rot set in and there was nothing he could do to prevent itchy soles and tinea between his toes. When he emerged relatively unscathed from the war, Johnson was rushed back into big cricket for Victoria and was picked in the one-off Test match against New Zealand in Wellington late in the summer of 1946. After the rigours of the jungle in New Guinea and other parts he found he couldn't stand wearing socks in hot weather. So when he turned out for either South Melbourne, Victoria or Australia he did so sockless. But if playing in New Zealand or England he put on a pair of thick woollen socks before slipping into his boots.

Johnson became Test captain in the mid 1950s – not the first that South Melbourne produced. There have been five others: Jack Blackham, Albert Trott, Warwick Armstrong, Bill Woodfull and Lindsay Hassett.

Johnson also holds another distinction in a longstanding Australian superstition. The number 87 is 'the devil's number' because it is 13 from a hundred. The superstition evolved during a conversation between Keith Miller and Johnson as they stood side by side in slips for South Melbourne. As they chatted Johnson said he got out for 87 once.

'Hey, Johnno, funny thing. I saw Don Bradman get out in a Sheffield Shield match at the MCG for 87,' Miller said with a laugh. But then Miller started to muse upon the number 87. Years ago I got wind of a sting in the tail about the legend, so I asked Miller if he knew something that most of us didn't know about the story.

'I used to go to the ground for the big matches to watch my heroes in action,' Miller said.

I was about 11 when I went to the MCG to see the mighty NSW team take on Victoria. It was December 27, 1929 and there was Bradman belting the hell out of the home attack. Then, out of the blue, Bradman chopped a ball on to his stumps from the fast bowler Harry 'Bull' Alexander. I looked at the scoreboard and it read Bradman bowled Alexander 87. I must have looked at the little scoreboard they used to have on the fence on both sides of the ground. It just read the incumbent batsmen and the last one out and their scores. So 87 became something in my mind. I used to read the newspapers and see how many 'unlucky' ones there were on Saturday club cricket and in the Shield and Test matches.' After the war players such as Richie Benaud, Alan Davidson and Norm O'Neill carried forward the legend that 87 was an unlucky number for the batsman. Once when SA batsman Les Favell reached 87 against NSW at the SCG, O'Neill sidled up to him and said, 'Hey, Les, look at the scoreboard. You are on 87.

Favell scoffed, then promptly got out for 87. When he walked to the crease in SA's second innings O'Neill again caught his ear: 'Hey Les, you are still on 87.' Poor Les got out for a duck.

But the legend that has endured – still does with cricketers Down Under – for generations was based on error. In the 1980s something stirred in Keith's memory and he checked the scoresheet of that 1929 match at the SCG library. There it read 'Bradman bowled Alexander 89.' Miller realised his error was all due to the MCG scoreboard not getting the score up quickly enough. He couldn't contact Ian Johnson fast enough.

'Hey Johnno remember our discussion in slips at South Melbourne about the "devil's number" before the war? Well you might have got out on 87, but Bradman actually made 89 that day.' Johnson put down the phone and stared out of the window, for he then realised he was an integral part of the legend that never was. However, despite the truth of the matter being disclosed, the number 87 is still the devil's number for many a batsman playing top cricket in Australia. Never let the truth get in the way of a good story.

Johnson played 45 Test matches – 17 of them as captain – hitting exactly 1000 runs at 18.51 with a highest score of 77. He took 109 wickets at 29.19. The highlight of his bowling career was his remarkable return against Wally Hammond's 1946–47 team at the SCG. Johnson bowled 30.1 overs operating his slow dipping, well-flighted deliveries into a stiff breeze and he completely mesmerised the Englishmen, taking a career best 6/42. It was during his reign as Test captain that Johnson was dubbed 'Myxomatosis' because he seemed to operate mainly when the lower-order 'rabbits' were at the crease.

His Test career ended in 1956, 10 years after it began, and in 1957 Johnson became secretary of the prestigious Melbourne Cricket Club, following in the footsteps of Hugh Trumble. Johnson had never smoked before he took up the position, but took to the pipe at his desk in the manner of Trumble.

It was at the MCG that I met Johnson. My first season with SA was in 1967–68 and some pundits reckoned I was a chance to tour England with the 1968 Australian team. The last Sheffield Shield match of the season was at the MCG and Sir Donald Bradman set up a meeting for me with Johnson. 'He'll give you some tips on bowling in different parts of the world,' said the Don with a smile. Johnson was terrific, imparting his knowledge. He spoke passionately about his under cutter, a ball I knew about by reading about him. It swerved away and kept going to defeat the batsman's outside edge but not the 'keeper. One day he had Bradman stumped with his under cutter. Johnson kept himself fit, at the age of 47 qualifying for a bronze medallion, which involved an ocean swim towing a bucket. At the age of 56, Johnson captained a team of old champions to Hong Kong for the last cricket match on that famous 125-year-old ground, which made way for Chater

Garden, which itself drew international attention in 2019, being the site of demonstrations in Hong Kong, as the large open space is conveniently opposite the parliament.

●

COLIN McCOOL

The quiet achiever

The influence of Don Bradman loomed large over the selection of the Australian team that toured England in 1948. Bradman knew he would have a glut of fast bowling talent in Ray Lindwall, Keith Miller and Bill Johnston, backed by the medium-fast Sam Loxton and off spinner Ian Johnson to play most of the Test matches. That a team could also take the new ball after only 55 overs inspired captains to utilise their faster bowlers more often than otherwise would have been the case. So the selectors, no doubt strongly swayed by captain Bradman, went for pace and for two slow leg spinners in Doug Ring and Colin McCool to run through the county sides to give the fast men a rest between Tests. There is no other conclusion to make about the spinners in the team, for SA's Bruce Dooland was far better than either Ring or McCool. George Tribe was arguably as good as them, if not better, and Cec Pepper, the best of the bunch, blotted his copybook by having a heated run-in with Bradman at the Adelaide Oval in 1946.

McCool was a short, strongly built chap who bowled flighted leg breaks and wrong'uns and batted in the middle to lower order with an array of shots square of the wicket – cuts and hooks – and he used his feet to the spinners. He was fortunate to tour England in 1948, but he didn't feature in Tests.

From 1956 to 1960 McCool played for Somerset in the English county championship, but he wasn't suited to the slow, low tracks in England. His high, floated deliveries were far better suited to the flint-hard wickets Down Under. McCool played seven times for his home state, NSW, before the war. After serving in the RAAF, McCool played for Queensland. He caught the attention of the Australian selectors in 1945–46 with a brilliant 6/36 against NSW, then 7/106 and a hard-hitting 172 against South Australia at Adelaide Oval. He followed up this fine form with 4/102 and 7/74 against the Australian Services team.

In the summer of 1946–47 McCool took 16 wickets for Queensland against Wally Hammond's MCC side before the first Test. In the first Test he hit 95. In the SCG second Test match he had a match haul of eight wickets, including 5/109. And at the MCG he scored a brilliant 104 not out, after coming to the wicket with Australia teetering on 5/188 and Norman Yardley on a hat-trick. He took 5/44 in the second England innings at the SCG in the fifth Test to round off a good series, finishing with a total of 18 wickets at 27.27, making him Australia's leading wickettaker with Ray Lindwall, and he scored 272 runs at an average of 54.50.

When he played at Somerset, McCool was portrayed as a 'thoughtful, but slightly aloof character'. After a day's play McCool would be seen sitting quietly by himself in a corner of the dressing-room smoking a pipe. English cricket writer Alan Gibson wrote of him:

> I think he (McCool) found some difficulty in accepting the conventions of English cricket as it was then. There was a Somerset committee member who liked and admired him and would

greet him with 'Morning McCool!' That committee member was seeking to be courteous, he would have thought it pompous to say, 'Mr McCool' and impertinent to say 'Colin'. But it infuriated Colin. He thought it a reflection on his status and would have preferred something like, 'Hi Col, you old bastard'. The worlds were too far apart.

In a total of 251 first-class matches McCool hit 12,421 runs at 32.88 with 18 centuries, a top score of 172. In addition he took 263 catches and effected two stumpings as stand-in wicketkeeper.

He married Dorothy Evelyn Yabsley in Sydney, in 1943. Their son, Russell, was born in Taunton and he played one first-class match for Somerset.

After his retirement from first-class cricket at the end of the 1960 county season McCool returned to Australia, taking up market gardening at Umina Beach on the Central Coast of NSW. He specialised in rare blooms.

McCool continued playing club cricket in the Newcastle competition for Belmont, however he was forced to quit the game altogether when rheumatism attacked his spinning fingers.

Colin Leslie McCool was renowned for his catching. Former teammate Bill O'Reilly paid tribute to Colin after his death in 1986, at the age of 69: 'If Colin had played in the last 10 years he would have been regarded as one of the greatest all-rounders in Australian cricket. He was a great batsman, a wonderful bowler and one of the best slips fieldsmen I have ever seen.'

CEC PEPPER

The unsung great one

Jack Fingleton wrote of the fabulous Australian all-rounder turned umpire, 'Cec Pepper looked like a cross between a Miami millionaire and an ice cream vendor.'

It was my first tour of England in 1968 and Australia was playing Surrey at The Oval. Cec Pepper was standing at the end from which I was bowling and it took only a couple of balls before he said with a laugh, 'You'll never die wondering, Rowdy. You always ask the question.' I did appeal a fair bit that day but there was no joy for me from Cec's end. But he was a great character. He probably didn't like giving away too many lbws after his brush with Don Bradman all those years before.

Cec played Sheffield Shield cricket for NSW from 1938–39 until 1940–41, whereupon he served in the Middle East and in New Guinea with the Australian Army, and was one of the first of the players to be selected for the Australian Services XI which took on England in the famous Victory Tests after the war.

It is said that there was never an angrier cricketer: 'rumbustious', as one writer put it. After the Victory Tests were over Pepper found himself in the Services side to play South Australia at Adelaide Oval. Don Bradman, at the age of 37, was making a tentative comeback. If he could get runs perhaps he might play another season or two after ill-health had forced him out of the army. On the field Pepper was no shrinking violet. He called it as he saw it. The whole cricket world wanted a big Bradman score; that is, those not in the field opposing him. Pepper reckoned he 'had the sod plumb lbw' twice within the space of two overs, but Umpire Jack Scott turned down each appeal. Sergeant Pepper of the Australian Services Team was enraged and he let go with a stream of vitriol aimed at Bradman, who complained to Scott, who in turn reported Pepper and that was effectively his last hurrah to make it in big cricket for Australia. In later years Pepper said he did send the Board a written apology for his outburst against Bradman, but the Board denied ever having received the letter.

Keith Miller reckoned Pepper was a mighty player and should have played in the 1948 Invincibles team, but Cec figured his future lay in playing cricket in England, as a professional in the Lancashire League.

Cecil George Pepper was born in the NSW mid-west town of Forbes on Sunday, 15 September 1918. He was a champion schoolboy cricketer, hitting more than 200 runs and taking more than 100 wickets for Parkes in one season.

While tennis was his first love and lured him to Sydney, it was as a cricketer that some eminent people saw his great potential. Sid Barnes, who in 1948 was in Bradman's Invincibles, helped Cec with accommodation while the youngster was making his name at the Petersham Cricket Club. He played just 16 first-class matches for

NSW, once grabbing 5/49 against South Australia in the 1939–40 summer, including the prize wicket of Bradman, caught for 40. After the war's end and his heroics with the Australian Services team, Cec really blew it with his exchange with Bradman.

In his later years Cec told Noel Wilde in the Lancashire Leagues history *The Greatest Show on Turf*:

> I always got on with Bradman, still do. But I got the little sod out twice in one innings and the umpire wouldn't give him out. When I told the umpire what I thought of his decisions I was expected to apologise (there and then). I wouldn't so I came to England.

Cec Pepper and Keith Miller stride to the wicket in a Lord's Cricket Ground Victory Test match, 1945. (PHOTO BY S&G/PA IMAGES VIA GETTY IMAGES)

Pepper didn't tour New Zealand with Bill Brown's Australian team at the end of that 1945–46 summer. Given that the selectors picked leg spinner Colin McCool and off spinner Ian Johnson, neither of whom were a patch on him, to go to NZ with O'Reilly, Cec Pepper could only have concluded his fate was sealed.

But like the stern schoolmaster who expels the brilliant student because of his attitude towards authority and then upon reflection lauds his old student, Bradman, years later, said: 'Cec was the second best spinner of my experience apart from O'Reilly. I couldn't pick the ball Cec bowled which somehow ducked in from outside off stump. It was not a wrong'un and not a flipper. It was a mystery to me.'

These flattering words came long after Pepper's Test aspirations had passed, buried in cricket history because of one angry outburst.

Cec played for a host of clubs in the Lancashire League and he became a legend. Years after belting sixes and taking wickets in the leagues, Cec announced that he was going to umpire county cricket in England.

His mates couldn't believe it. This after all was the man who by mutual agreement with his captain Jock Livingston left the Commonwealth team's tour of India in 1950–51 early 'because those bloody umpires wind me up too much'.

So it came to pass that Cec Pepper became a first-class cricket umpire on the county circuit in England at the start of the 1964 season. He laughed and traded verbal abuse with the players for 16 summers and he brought his own brand of justice to the pitch. Pepper may well have been the cricketing equivalent of the hanging judge. He dressed flamboyantly in black trousers, white coat and the loudest pair of spats since those seen during the tap-dancing days of Gene Kelly and Fred Astaire.

Cec would say of county captains who were so often cosseted, pampered to the extreme: 'I used to shoot 'em out, no matter who they were.'

Never one to hold back, Cec was once quizzed about the ability of England all-rounder Ian Botham. 'Botham? The world's best all-rounder? He wouldn't have got in the NSW dressing-room in my day. I could have bowled him out with a cabbage, with the leaves on.'

Cec Pepper was the great spinner Australian cricket ignored, and the England establishment at Lord's could not bring itself to grant him a chance to stand as an umpire in a Test match. Pepper left the game in 1979 because he felt 'certain umpires' were gifted their Test spots.

Sadly, gone was his dream of standing in a Test match with fellow Australian Bill Alley at Lord's. Despite a lifetime in cricket, he never got to play or umpire a single Test.

Although Pepper often shot himself in the foot, he was also sensitive, with a joyous, sometimes outrageous, sense of humour. He never tired of talking spin, showing how, with his long fingers, he spun the leg break, the top-spinner, wrong'un and flipper. It gave him great joy to impart his knowledge of the spinning art to young and old and he was ever giving, never dismissive.

His life away from cricket hardly lacked for spice, for Pepper lived in a ménage à trois and he willed half his fortune to a woman he'd just met.

This wonderful cricketer was greatly misunderstood as a man and sadly remains largely unsung in the annals of the game.

DOUG RING

Ever the bridesmaid

Doug Ring was a burly, almost rotund, leg spinner who could hit out willingly with the bat. He played 13 Test matches, taking 35 wickets at 37.28, and was a member of Don Bradman's 1948 Invincibles, but did not play a Test until the fifth one at The Oval, Bradman's farewell. Bradman, of course, made a duck; for his part Ring scored 9 batting at number 10 and took 1/44 off 28 overs.

He bowled a good leg break and for variety a useful slider, rather than the conventional top-spinner, which generally bounces a good deal. Ring's slider was released out the front of his hand, the ball angling in to the right-hander and skipping off the wicket straight and low. He taught the young Richie Benaud to bowl this ball when on the England tour with the Australians in 1953. Doug also learned to bowl a flipper, which was passed on to him by his Richmond captain-coach Les Keating. If the ball was propelled seam up when it landed it might dart in or away.

He had a couple of great days in the sun, taking 6/72 against South Africa in 1952–53 and 6/80 versus the West Indies in 1951–52.

That innings he dismissed Clyde Walcott, Frank Worrell and the Windies captain John Goddard. Ring was useful with the bat. That series he hit 65 at the SCG, 67 at Adelaide and a stirring unbeaten 32 to grab the lion's share of a 38-run last-wicket stand with Bill Johnston to snatch victory at the MCG.

In all first-class matches Ring took 451 wickets at 28.48, taking five wickets or more an innings on 21 occasions and 10 or more wickets in a game twice. He played his last Test at The Oval in 1953, sailed home and joined the public service where he worked for 30-odd years. Doug also commentated on the game on TV. No doubt he suffered from the glut of fast bowlers in his era and the new ball being taken after but 55 overs, in comparison to 80 these days. Pity. Had Doug Ring played in today's cricket where batsmen are anchored to the crease and rarely work the ball into gaps to break the rhythm of the bowler, he might have become one of the very best wrist spinners. His 13 Tests came over a period of six years. There were a lot of first-class matches for Victoria in the Sheffield Shield competition and on tour in the minor matches before and after the Tests. In a sense he was ever the bridesmaid.

GEORGE TRIBE

'He'd run under a bus to take a catch'

Around 2007 fellow spin bowler Terry Jenner and I were putting a group of young spinners through their paces at Adelaide Oval No 2 ground when a little bloke turned up and asked if he could have a bowl.

We reckoned he was well into his eighties at the time.

'I'll have to bowl from about 15 yards fellas,' he laughed. 'Bit of arthritis in the left shoulder.'

We could immediately clearly see the bloke had once been a fine bowler. He bowled left-hand Chinaman stuff and he gave the ball a bit of a rip.

After three balls of good line and dipping flight he thrust out his right hand: 'George Tribe ... just here for a couple of days. You may have heard my name here and there. I played a Test or two for Australia, but most of my cricket was in England. I played league cricket then county cricket.'

George was another of those whose careers were forestalled by WWII. He was briefly called up to serve in the army, but he was

113

discharged within a few months because of his qualification as an engineer, a so-called reserved occupation.

His three Tests came against Wally Hammond's touring 1945–46 team, which yielded him but two wickets. The last of those Tests turned out to be his last game in Australia. He then accepted an offer to play for Milnrow in the Central Lancashire League. The money in those days could be substantial – in fact, greater than a Test player's pay packet for an entire Ashes tour of England. It was assumed he would return to Australia and to Test cricket; apparently Bradman had hinted as much. However George's family circumstances changed everything. His wife gave birth to twins during the northern summer and he decided to stay in Britain. Tribe was hugely successful in Lancashire League cricket with Milnrow and Rawtenstall.

After five years he had qualified to play county cricket and his friend and fellow Australian Jock Livingston, who had captained him on the Commonwealth tour of India, recommended Tribe to the Northamptonshire County Cricket Club.

On that India tour he'd taken 99 wickets at 17.5 – more than double the number of wickets of the next best bowler. According to fellow spinner Jim Laker,

> When George's appeals for lbw against a maharajah were continually turned down, he lifted the umpire, who was tiny, even smaller than George, into the air and shouted, 'Don't be such a bloody fool. Have another look!' The tiny ump reconsidered on the spot and quickly raised his right index finger. Ah, justice for the Tribe.

Immediately after he was signed by Northants, Tribe landed a job to carry him through the winter months. A cricket-loving supporter of the club, John Pascoe, ran the engineering firm British

Timken and saw to it that Tribe was given seniority, which carried a good pay packet. Financial security was assured.

Playing Lancashire League cricket was good in terms of a season-by-season contract, plus what money a player could pick up on the side. Hit a six to bring up your 50 and they took a bucket around the ground for fans to donate. Similarly a five-wicket haul and round the ground an official went to accept donations.

These collections were normal for all the clubs and the players loved them. George could hit a six or two and he always bagged more than his share of wickets. From the outset George was feted by Northamptonshire. He enjoyed eight full seasons for Northants, doing the 1000/100 double seven times. In 1955 he took 176 wickets in the season and was named as one of the Five Cricketers of the Year in *Wisden Cricketers' Almanack*.

At Northants he played alongside wicketkeeper Keith Andrew, who described Tribe as 'probably the best cricketer I ever played with'. Frank Tyson regarded Australia's neglect of George Tribe as 'criminal'.

George had begun his cricketing life as a left-arm finger spinner, but changed to becoming a wrist spinner in the wake of the 1937 change in the lbw law that allowed the batsman being given out to a ball pitching outside the off stump and spinning back to hit the stumps. George bowled a quickish straight one that scurried off the pitch low like a thief in the night. It was the George Tribe 'squibber'!

The English batsmen were often mesmerised by his dipping flight and sharp spin. One day he beat the Kent and England batsman Colin Cowdrey's outside edge six balls in a row at Tunbridge Wells. Cowdrey must have died a thousand deaths at the indignity of it all. There was more than a hint of the Clarrie Grimmett cunning in that George would ensure that players such as Tom Graveney were 'given' a single so he could go to town on the rabbits. Not an elegant batsman, Tribe was nonetheless effective. His teammates called him 'tripod', because when dragging the ball to cow corner he would end up with his bat splayed on the ground like a third leg.

He became a legend of the Northamptonshire County Cricket Club. Tribe gave the club belief. In 1955 he took a record 176 championship wickets and in 1956 he destroyed a strong Yorkshire batting side at Wantage Road, Northampton, taking a match haul of 15/31 (7/22 and 8/9) – a club record.

Richie Benaud said of Tribe's fielding: 'He would run under a bus to take a catch ...' – insert the famous Benaud pause '... off his own bowling!'

Before leaving for England, George played Australian Rules football for Footscray (now the Bulldogs) in the Victorian Football League, playing 66 matches between 1940 and 1946. A small forward, he kicked 80 goals. He was just the opportunist and seemed to possess what they call in the game, 'goal sense'. His brother Tom went on to play 101 games for the Bulldogs.

George's two wickets in three Tests at an average of 165 do not look impressive, but his first-class career reads otherwise. Overall in 308 first-class games for NSW and Northants, he took 1378 wickets at 20.55. He achieved a strike rate of 46.1 and took five wickets in an innings 93 times and 10 wickets in a match on 23 occasions.

George Tribe was a charming, generous soul. He was the very epitome of a cricket enthusiast. Often when seeing a bunch of children playing cricket on the street or in a field, he would stop his car to coach them. Despite his generosity and sense of paying things forward in the game, George never lost his competitive streak. When he returned to Australia in 1959, taking up a role in the Australian branch of the UK engineering firm British Timken, he captained Yarraville, the club where he'd started as a 15-year-old all those years before. When he was well into his fifties George took 5/8 against a media team before he was taken off. 'Pity, I was just about to make you blokes look a bit ordinary!'

As he lay in care at the age of 88, George was asked if he had any final requests. 'Yes, I want to play cricket with the boys on the hill.'

THE BENAUD ERA

Richie Benaud stood head and shoulders above the pack as the leading Australian spinner from late 1956. He toured England in 1953 and in 1956 with little impact; it was in South Africa in the summer of 1957–58 that he made his mark.

There seemed a myriad spinners in the era. When Benaud wasn't about for NSW there was Fred Johnson and Bob Roxby. Queensland had Brian Flynn for a time, then along came NSW-born Wal Walmsley, a journeyman leg spinner who went from Sydney to Brisbane, then played and coached in Tasmania before heading to the Lancashire League, following the time-honoured trek for spinners not making the Test scene Down Under. NSW fielded two spinners in Sheffield Shield matches – Benaud and the left-arm Chinaman merchant Johnny Martin. They formed a terrific spin partnership over a long time.

NSW leggie Peter Philpott did well for a time, playing eight Tests, but his figures didn't reflect his ability. He took just 26 wickets at 38.46, with one day in the sun against England in 1965, taking 5/90.

Victorian left-arm orthodox spinner Ian Quick made the 1961 tour of England, but didn't excel on wickets that many had thought he might.

Left-arm Chinaman bowler Lindsay Kline fared pretty well in a limited number of Tests, distinguishing himself with a hat-trick at Cape Town against South Africa in the summer of 1957–58. Lindsay, always known as 'Spinner', was also there at the end in the first Tied Test – against West Indies at Brisbane in 1960–61. Then there was the sensational left-arm Chinaman bowler David Sincock, who spun so sharply. Tony Lock, who played for England, was a big figure in the local game, getting the fledgling WA state team to mix it with the eastern staters. Queensland off spinner Tom Veivers made batsmen earn their runs, and the Indian-born South Australian Rex Sellers might have carved a great Test career, but for damaged ligaments in his spinning fingers. He played one Test against India on the way home from the Test tour of England in 1964. But really, this period of spin was dominated by just one man ...

RICHIE BENAUD

Homespun magic

Born in the shadow of the Blue Mountains at Penrith on 6 October 1930, Richie inherited his father's love of cricket. In the summer of 1922–23 his leg spinning father, Lou, took all 20 wickets for 65 runs playing for Penrith Waratahs against St Marys. In 1940, at the age of 10, young Richie went with his father to see a match at the Sydney Cricket Ground for the first time. NSW was pitted against South Australia, and the youngster was about to witness cricket history – and the consequences of the day would echo down the years.

Clarrie Grimmett was the one who caught his eye. Grimmett had long wanted to unleash his latest creation, the flipper, which he had started working on about the time Richie was born. Grimmett didn't want to expose the ball to the world until he had mastered all aspects of the delivery.

The time had come. Grimmett had indeed perfected his new specialty. It looks like a leg break, but it isn't. Flicked straight out of the hand, with backspin on the ball, it hits the pitch and goes straight on, faster, skidding, putting the unwary batsman in danger of being bowled or dismissed lbw.

'For more than ten years I worked on my new mystery ball before I could control it perfectly,' Clarrie told me decades later, in the early 1970s.

> After all that time I decided to bowl it in a match. The Test opener Sid Barnes told everyone that he could pick my flipper, the ball that turned out to be my greatest delivery. Barnes had been talking a lot about his success in picking the flipper, but as far as I could remember I had not even bowled it to him.

Barnes was that sort of character, a wheeler and dealer. He must have heard about the mystery ball, and gone on the attack by declaring he already knew how to pick it.

> The NSW batsmen came in and I was in a bit of a state, wondering and doubting the wisdom of using the flipper. It wasn't lack of confidence in pitching it exactly where I intended, I just questioned whether I should bowl it in this game. But I was very keen to show Barnes up. As I went back to bowl, I was tossing up whether to test him. As I ran to the wicket I thought I would this very ball and over went the flipper. It cut through and left Barnes right in front lbw. (Arthur) Chipperfield came in next so I turned it on him and he too went plumb lbw.

After witnessing the brilliance of Grimmett on the sacred turf that is the SCG, young Richie Benaud went home with wings on his feet. He was elated. All thought of bowling off-breaks was suddenly off the radar; from now on, leg spin it would be.

Under his father's watch Richie developed a fizzing leg break, with lots of top spin, a good top-spinner and the wrong'un. The flipper would have to wait. Richie's secondary education was at

Parramatta High School and he made his first-grade debut with Cumberland at the age of 16. At that stage of his career he was a batsman who bowled a bit. In November 1948 Richie was picked for NSW Colts, scoring an unconquered 47 and taking 3/37 in his side's innings defeat of Queensland. His first-class career began at the age of 19 for NSW versus Queensland in the New Year's match of the 1948–49 summer. Rain spoiled his chances of bowling and he scored just two runs. Getting any game at the time for NSW was almost like a leap onto the Test stage, for that summer with all the Test players available, the likes of Benaud and the other untried had to bide their time for a chance. Benaud was relegated to the second XI and in the match against Victoria on the MCG he suffered a terrible blow to the head from an attempted hook by a ball from Victorian medium pacer Jack Daniel. After 28 X-rays that revealed nothing, the final diagnosis was that the crater in his forehead had resulted in a skull fracture and Richie was sidelined from playing cricket for the rest of the season. He spent two weeks in hospital for the surgery.

The next summer he was again picked for NSW and in the Shield match against South Australia in Adelaide he belted 93. Richie had won a place in the side when Keith Miller was called up to the Test team as a replacement for Bill Johnston, who was injured in a motor accident on the tour of South Africa. The unpredictable but brilliant Miller had a lasting impact on Benaud, both as a player and as a leader. Richie saw Miller take chances as a captain, with a seeming careless attitude, but he gleaned that under that façade of nonchalance there lay a superb cricketing brain. When Miller led NSW on to the field he would often grab the ball and when at the top of his approach would yell 'scatter!' Miller had a golden way about him: his men knew their positions in the field and they appreciated his total faith in their abilities. One time after leading the players on to the field someone said to him, 'Keith, there are twelve of us on the field.' Without the slightest hesitation, Miller said: 'Will one of you blokes piss off?'

Miller soon realised the amazing raw talent in the young Benaud and batted him as high as possible in the order for NSW.

While Bradman had retired from the game, the Test side still had an impressive look about it. The attack comprised Ray Lindwall, Miller and Bill Johnston, with off spinner Ian Johnson. For a while there was the sensational finger-flick spinner Jack Iverson. But like a shooting star Iverson's brilliance was only with us for what seemed like the blinking of an eye. Victorian leg spinner Doug Ring was the incumbent number one spinner for 13 Test matches, but his 35 wickets were proving costly. After some good efforts with the bat, although still inconsistent with his leg breaks, Benaud was picked to play in the fifth Test against the West Indies at the SCG in 1950–51, as the second spinner to Ring. The Victorian returned 1/44 off 13 overs and Richie, from 4.3 overs took 1/14. Benaud had the great Windies batsman Everton Weekes dropped by wicketkeeper Gil Langley, and his first Test wicket was left-arm spinner and tailender Alf Valentine.

Bradman could see the great all-round potential in Benaud and envisioned great things of him as a leader. Benaud won selection in the Australian tour of England in 1953 under the affable Lindsay Hassett, but the young man did little of note in the Tests. His best with the bat was 7 in four completed innings and his best return with the ball was 1/51 off 17 overs in the Lord's second Test. He took just two Test wickets at an average of 87 runs apiece. A blazing 135 with 11 sixes in 110 minutes against TN Pearce's XI at Scarborough, one of the last matches of the tour, gave the Australian selectors new heart.

They stuck by Benaud. On the next tour, in 1956, when Jim Laker ran amok on dusty, spin-friendly wickets, Australia won just one Test, at Lord's. In that match Benaud hit a brilliant 97 in 113 balls as if to announce his coming stardom to the cricketing gods in the House of Lords. A highlight was a hooked six into the grandstand off a Freddie Trueman bouncer.

On his 21st birthday he became engaged to Marcia Lavener, with whom he once worked in an accountant's office. In the Sydney Test of 1952–52 South Africa's John Waite cut hard and Richie, a brilliant gully fieldsman, lost sight of the ball in the backdrop of the crowd and received a nasty gash to his upper lip. He had the injury treated, and was back on the field before the Test was over, taking two wickets with his leg breaks – although appealing through his cut lip was difficult. Six days later Richie married Marcia, managing to mumble the two words that mattered most. The celebratory drinks were had through a straw. The couple had two children, Gregory and Jeffrey.

After Ian Johnson retired, the Test selectors overlooked both the favourite Neil Harvey and the outside chance Benaud in favour of 22-year-old Ian Craig for the Test captaincy, and to lead the 1957–58 tour of South Africa. Australia had lost three successive Ashes series and the selectors were looking for rejuvenation. Craig, who had made the youngest ever first-class debut aged 18, was now the nation's youngest captain.

Until that tour Richie was teetotal. He went straight from the field to a shower, then dinner and the theatre or cinema. All this changed in the series against the Springboks. Cricketers past and present came into the Australian dressing-room at day's end and the players would sit and drink beer and yarn about the game – and Benaud listened and learned.

Benaud batted and bowled brilliantly in this series. It was as if a cloud had lifted, leaving his career bathed in God's sunshine, in favour with the cricketing gods. In 18 first-class games on the tour Benaud bowled in excess of 6000 balls, taking 106 wickets and hitting four centuries, two of them in Tests. Staying at the ground to have a beer and a yarn with his teammates was important to his future chances of becoming the Test captain.

By the time England arrived in Australia for the Ashes series of 1958–59, Craig was forced out of the team and the captaincy through illness. The selectors, having ignored Harvey and Benaud in the past, had to select a new Australian captain and fast. Neil Harvey led an Australian XI against Peter May's MCC team in Sydney and Benaud, who had led NSW twice only in three years, had to be content with leading Cumberland in grade games.

With Craig sidelined, it was between Harvey and Benaud, with most pundits betting on Harvey to get the job. After the Australian XI match, which Harvey's men lost heavily courtesy of Tony Lock's 6/29 in the second dig, Harvey answered the phone in his Sydney office.

'Guess who is the new Australian captain?'

'You are!'

'That's right, Nin,' (a shortened version of Neil's nickname, Ninna) Benaud said. 'I am sorry, mate. I thought you should have got it.'

Harvey kept his disappointment to himself. He embraced Benaud's appointment with enthusiasm. The pair lunched together at the NSW Cricketers' Club and chatted over a few drinks. He told Richie that he would have been very annoyed if the captaincy was given to anyone else but him and that he would give him his total and unconditional support and loyalty.

Harvey later wrote:

Richie brought a spirit of vitality and vigour into the Australian side. Apart from proving a keen on-field tactician, Richie managed to cultivate team morale better than any captain I have played under. He brought with him new ideas and quickly moulded his side into the happiest cricketing unit imaginable.

Benaud introduced team dinners for the players before every Test match. He invited all members of the team to contribute to tactical discussion. Australia won the series 4–0. Benaud had come of age as a spinner and proved his mettle as Test captain. The late 1950s had been a time of doldrums for Test cricket. Negative tactics abounded. The crowds stayed away in droves. But Benaud was putting an end to all that – and restoring the winning habit. A tour of Pakistan and India followed, with 2–0 and 2–1 victories recorded. Now it was time for Benaud's crowning glory, the 1960–61 visit by the West Indies.

At tea on the fifth day in the first Test at the Gabba, Australia needed 130 runs with three wickets in hand. As the players walked off, Sir Donald Bradman said to Benaud: 'What are your thoughts?'

'We are going for a win.'

'Good to hear it,' Sir Donald smiled.

The runs came thick and fast after tea. Benaud and Alan Davidson had a rollicking century-plus partnership and seemed certain to win the game themselves. With Australia cruising at 6/226, Benaud dropped the ball at his feet and called for a run. Davidson reacted swiftly, but little Joe Solomon at mid-wicket swooped, grabbed the ball and threw down the wicket with Davo stranded: Australia 7/226, still seven runs to win. Davo said later, 'even Usain Bolt would have struggled to make his ground'.

Two runs later Benaud hooked at a Wes Hall bouncer, got a glove and Gerry Alexander gleefully took the catch behind: 8/228. Five runs needed. Ian Meckiff somehow scraped together two runs. By the last over three runs were required for victory. Wally Grout negotiated a few balls, then he hooked a Hall bouncer, the ball soaring to the mid-wicket boundary. It seemed a certain four, but Conrad Hunte had other ideas. He chased the ball down and threw magnificently to the end Grout was running. Grout was well out of his ground when the bails were removed: Australia 9/232. In walked

Lindsay Kline, the man they called 'Spinner'. Two balls left. One run needed. Spinner decided to push and run. He dug the attempted yorker out and ran. Meckiff scampered towards the batting end, but he didn't count on Solomon at mid-wicket. Solomon had honed his throwing skills knocking mangoes out of trees in his home town of Port Mourant, Berbice, in what was then British Guiana, on the northern coast of South America. The ball had slewed from the bottom of Kline's bat to just in front of square where Peter Lashley was about to field the ball.

Suddenly Solomon, the mid-wicket specialist, appeared. 'Out the way, Pete, move, move, it's mine.' Solomon grabbed the ball cleanly and threw down the stumps side-on with Meckiff out of his ground. Result: the first Tied Test in history. Not one of the previous 487 Tests had ended this way.

Bradman wore a grin from ear to ear. Here was an Australian cricket team on the attack. And here was a West Indian team with a like purpose. Australia's Richie Benaud and the West Indian captain Frank Worrell created the environment for a great series. Attack was the key, with bat, ball and in the field.

Bizarrely Alan McGilvray, arguably the greatest ball-by-ball commentator the ABC has produced, didn't stay at the ground to watch the finish of the match. He left the Gabba to catch an early flight to Sydney. He had apparently given Australia no chance of winning the game.

Benaud led his men to England in 1961, but fibrositis of his bowling shoulder preventing him from playing in the second Test at Lord's. Neil Harvey led the side, his first and only Test match as captain. Davidson promised Harvey a big effort and he took 5/42 in the England first innings of 206. Bill Lawry hit a courageous 130 against the England attack on the infamous Lord's Ridge, setting up an Australian win with debutant Graham McKenzie taking 5/37 off 29 overs in the England second innings. Benaud returned for the

Richie Benaud preparing to bat in 1963. (AUSTRALIAN NEWS AND INFORMATION BUREAU, PHOTOGRAPHER W PEDERSEN)

third Test at Leeds and lost badly, Yorkshireman Freddie Trueman enjoying a match haul of 11/88 (5/58 and 6/30). At Old Trafford England was in the box seat on the last day. Wanting 256 runs to win in 230 minutes, Geoff Pullar and Raman Subba Row went for them early to signal that the chase was on.

Benaud attacked with his field placings, even when Ted Dexter was in full flight.

Dexter was a brilliant, almost aristocratic stroke-maker and was in total control when, on 76, he cut hard at a Benaud leg break that bounced and the Englishman succeed only in snicking the ball into the safe gloves of Wally Grout. The pitch was still a beauty for batting, but there were a few rough patches outside the right-hander's leg stump. Benaud decided to play on the batsmen's nerves.

Given the runs were made so quickly for the loss of Puller (26) and Dexter (76), England was still well on track to win comfortably. Then came the ball of the match to get Peter May. Benaud bowled it outside the right-hander's leg stump. It landed in the rough and bowled the England captain round his legs. Benaud finished with 6/70 off 32 overs and Australia had won a famous victory. Benaud's policy of all-out attack paid off handsomely. Australia won the series 2–1 and the Ashes were retained by Benaud's men.

When Richie retired from Test cricket at the end of the 1963–64 summer, he had scored 2201 runs at 24.46 with three centuries and nine fifties. He wheeled down 19,108 balls in Tests, taking 248 wickets at 27.03. And he took 65 catches. His captaincy had changed the game of cricket – and his influence over it had only just begun.

When Kerry Packer launched his revolutionary World Series Cricket in the 1970s, Benaud was its public face: the man in the beige jacket in the commentary box. Many in the know believed his hand was the most influential in its success. His calmness under intense pressure made some of the old hands in television marvel.

Packer chose Ian Chappell to lead his Australian side, and Chappell was to spend many years alongside Benaud in the Channel Nine box.

'Whether it was in business or cricket or life in general, he (Benaud) was the person I always approached,' Ian Chappell once told me.

Chappell's association with Benaud began much earlier. In 1963 soon after Chappell had scored his maiden first-class century – 149 versus Benaud's NSW at Adelaide Oval – he travelled to England to play a season of Lancashire League. When he arrived at the Ramsbottom Club, there awaiting him was a new Gray-Nicolls cricket bat, courtesy of one Richie Benaud.

Benaud could foresee Chappell as a Test player of the future. He knew how tough it was for players of that era to have to fork out money for all their equipment. The state associations provided a sleeveless jumper, a long-sleeved jumper and a cap. That was it. Even the Test players had to buy their own gear. A bat had to be bought, so too boots, creams, shirts. The player even had to pay for his own dry-cleaning. State and Test cricketers played a lot of club cricket in those days – where they were expected to pay ball fees every Saturday. Yes, they paid to play. Chappell appreciated that bat.

Rich was always generous of spirit to emerging players and always made time to help a young bowler or journalist.

He worked for a Sydney tabloid newspaper as a journalist. He was a proper, proficient journalist covering all manner of events, not just cricket: local council affairs, parliament, police rounds, feature articles. It didn't make his move into television seamless; what made his move brilliant was his staying behind in London after the 1956 Australian tour and undergoing a three-week commentators' course with the BBC.

His philosophy of 'less is more' towards television commentary was brilliant. Richie believed that a commentator should not say a word unless he could add to the images. As he put it, 'Don't tell them what they are seeing; tell them what they don't see.' He was master of the pause. Sometimes his silence said it all. Even today, years after his death, anyone who follows the game in this country can only think of Richie when the score hits 222 – 'two, two, two'.

It is by now a longstanding tradition that dozens of blokes turn up to the SCG Test dressed as Richie Benaud. They have wigs of greying blond hair and wear the Benaud beige jacket. Each man carries a microphone bearing the Channel Nine logo. Richie was well aware of the Richies. Richie is gone now – but the Richies keep coming.

In the Australian summer of 1968–69 I was 12th man for the fifth Test at the SCG. Bill Lawry's team won the match and Rich had no doubt been in the Windies dressing-room occupied by both teams sharing a drink, as was tradition after the last day of a series.

As Rich was about to leave he noticed me by the window. He stopped and said, 'A tour of India is a most important part of a young Australian cricketer's education.' How right he was: the cricket challenges of spinning wickets, the umpiring, the poor-quality accommodation in those days, extreme weather and fanatical spectators all added up. But I loved the spinning wickets. I managed 28 wickets at 19 runs apiece; the record wicket tally for an Australian bowler in a Test series in India is 29, held jointly by Alan Davidson and Richie Benaud. I was glad not to have bettered their record. They were my heroes and I'm happy to sit in behind them.

In the early 1960s Richie married pretty Derbyshire brunette Daphne Surfleet. Daphne proved to be an amazing secretarial support to author EM Swanton during his penning of the 600,000-word epic *The World of Cricket*. Daphne studied the game of cricket, knew the game inside out and had a brilliant memory. She was a terrific organiser and was the personal assistant to team assistant manager

Fred Bennett for the 1972 Ashes tour. I had a suspicion that Daphne was doing all the work and Fred was going along for the ride.

On that 1972 tour I got to know the Benauds better. During matches in London, Richie and Daphne were to be found at the Knightsbridge flat of their friends, John and Dumpy Morley. They were grand hosts and often had a few of the Australians to a Sunday roast when the team was in town. The Benauds knew a wide range of people from all walks of life in Australia, England, South Africa, West Indies and New Zealand. John Morley was but one of them, an antique dealer whose pride and joy was a blue Ferrari, which he enjoyed driving rather fast. One day up north he was clocked by two Yorkshire policemen at 170 miles per hour (270 km/h). The police

A fine gathering in England, 1972. From left: Ashley Mallett, Ray Steele, Richie Benaud, Allan McGilvray and the former British Prime Minister, Sir Alec Douglas-Hume. (ASHLEY MALLETT COLLECTION)

gave up the chase and they decided to take a slip road, for one knew a good pub nearby and, as they were out of their jurisdiction, a few beers would go down a treat.

Just as they approached the pub car-park they noticed a distinctive blue Ferrari parked near the front entrance. They rushed into the pub and one announced, 'Who owns the blue Ferrari out front?'

'I do,' Morley said confidently.

Both policemen walked towards Morley, thrust out their hands and one said with a big smile: 'Congratulations, that's the first time we've caught someone going 100 miles per hour over the speed limit.' They helped John celebrate by shouting him a couple of pints. Different times.

The Australian players found Daphne an absolute delight, and she sent back to Australia all manner of correspondence and recorded tapes for our families. Rich and Daphne enjoyed the company of the Australian players. They enjoyed the characters, the brilliance of some and the mayhem of others.

They particularly enjoyed my clumsiness.

On the morning of the first one-day international at Lord's, Rich offered to help me in the nets. I had developed a bad habit of running on the wicket on my follow-through. Unfortunately I had had a few too many at the previous night's team dinner and was a bit the worse for wear when I met Rich in the nets. I suspect my immediate improvement was due partly to Rich's inspiration and partly to a stumble or two left into the safety of the practice net.

England won the toss and batted. I fielded at third man and Geoffrey Boycott guided one down through the gully. I had the ball in my sights, but there was a slight misjudgement: I ran right and the ball stayed left.

There were a few other instances of clumsiness, including walking through the stumps when retrieving my cap from the umpire, which would have raised a wry smile from Rich and

Daphne. After 12 overs I had 2/24: Man of the Match award stuff ... if Chappelli had let me bat first drop.

Richie, of course, was always immaculately dressed, never a hair out of place. Whenever I was with him he'd always find something wrong on me, such as a tie askew.

One day I thought I'd be absolutely beyond reproach. I'd had my suit dry-cleaned, shirt laundered, new shoes ... just for the Sydney Test match.

I saw Rich in the distance and confidently approached.

He smiled generously and thrust out his hand.

Then, to my utter horror, he pointed to the middle of my tie and there it was ... a tomato pip.

Some things never change.

The year was 1976. Australia had just beaten Clive Lloyd's West Indians 5–1 on home soil. In March of that year Richie Benaud was the manager of the International Wanderers tour of South Africa. Benaud had brought the team to the republic to help South Africa's non-white cricketers and to help break down barriers. In accordance with Benaud's stipulation the team included a number of non-white cricketers – Tiffie Barnes, Winston Carelse, Baboo Ebrahim, Devdas Govindjee, David Jacobs and Farouk Timol.

We won the first match in Cape Town, drew the second in Johannesburg and lost the final match in Durban, thanks to an inspirational bowling performance by the left-arm spinner Baboo Ebrahim.

The Australians on the tour had become acquainted with Ebrahim six years earlier, when he had turned up to the Australian team's training and asked if he could bowl to Lawry's men. Ian Redpath, who was Lawry's opening partner, told the young Ebrahim that he could. A burly white security guard thought otherwise. 'He can't bowl to your men. That man is black.' Ebrahim did bowl to the Australians – and immediately impressed. He was better than the two spinners South Africa played in that Test match, off spinner Michael Seymour and left-armer Grahame Chevalier.

Baboo's performance in the third unofficial Test in Durban in 1976 warmed the hearts of all, even the Wanderers. He took six second-innings wickets to humble our side.

One teammate was the jovial West Indian and Kent all-rounder John Shepherd. He particularly agonised over Ebrahim. Here was a brilliantly gifted spinner denied the chance to play for his country in an official Test match because of the colour of his skin. For the duration of our short tour, Benaud insisted there be no restrictions on where people, regardless of colour, could stand or sit to watch a game. He also stipulated that bars in all parts of the ground be open to people of all races and colours. By contrast, in 1970 when the Australian team had played its first provincial match of the tour in Pretoria, no non-white person was permitted to enter the ground.

In Johannesburg Benaud had booked the team into a restaurant for a meal. Everyone was neatly, albeit casually, dressed: slacks, open-necked shirt and sports coat. The restaurant manager approached a table and began an extraordinary tirade where John Shepherd was sitting.

'Get out,' he yelled at Shep. 'No tie, no service. You are not welcome here. Leave the premises immediately.'

Incensed, Benaud confronted the restaurant manager. 'Don't concern yourself. We are all leaving and we plan to eat at a civilised establishment.'

Whether the tour achieved any lasting good for the non-whites of the republic is debatable. Apartheid was a such a dreadful, heartless policy that only a concerted effort by many within and without the country could ever overturn minority rule. Eventually protests over many years, trade sanctions, isolation and international sporting ostracism prevailed.

However, the International Wanderers tour demonstrated to the masses – black and white – through Baboo Ebrahim's bowling in Durban, that a black South African was as good as and, in Baboo's case, better than, a white man in the game of cricket. They knew that already, of course.

Richie Benaud influenced cricket and cricketers after WWII more than any other person, including Bradman. Young cricketers, emerging journalists, would-be commentators – he had them all in the palm of his hand. Just like the flipper he bowled so handsomely, after Bruce Dooland showed him how to bowl it, after its creator Clarrie Grimmett had shown him – which would in turn be bowled soon enough by one Shane Keith Warne.

The eminent lyricist and writer – and my good friend – Sir Tim Rice, over a glass of wine in Tasmania, once asked Benaud if he would consider becoming MCC president at cricket headquarters, Lord's Cricket Ground. Richie politely declined.

> I wanted him to know that the Marylebone club, a conservative pillar of the England cricket Establishment, which curiously I was representing in 2002–03, could have imagined no greater honour than having Richie – an Australian hero whose progressive views on the game both on and off the field for so many years had been so instrumental in dragging the game into each successive era – at its helm.

Richie Benaud brought his special magic to the game of cricket.

●

LINDSAY KLINE

'Come in, Spinner'

Lindsay Kline bowled left-arm Chinaman wrist spin with a high arm, higher than the usual run of wristies. The high arm gave him a lot of bounce, but it also negated his ability to get much turn back into the right-hander. His wrong'un was his best ball and he often used it to telling effect. A gentle man with a fabulous sense of humour, Lindsay was called 'Spinner', an apt nickname for any man of spin, but the name became uniquely his and it was used so extensively in a number of countries that people weren't sure about his given first name. No matter, Spinner it became and Spinner it was forevermore.

On 1 February 1961, as Australian wickets tumbled to the West Indian attack on the last day of the fourth Test at Adelaide Oval, Norm O'Neill and 12th man Johnny Martin took the team's No 11, Spinner Kline, to the nets at the back of the George Giffen Stand, for what they hoped would be a confidence-boosting net.

For the next 15 minutes, Martin and O'Neill, a champion batsman and part-time spinner, continually clean bowled Spinner, who hardly got a bat to ball. So bad was his effort that a woman watching at the back of the net yelled, 'You're hopeless Kline. Waste of time you going out there.'

When Des Hoare was clean bowled by Frank Worrell for a duck the score stood at 9/207. The hope of the side gathered his gloves, pulled on his baggy green and made his way down the steps through a throng of SACA members. One of them yelled in jest, 'Won't be long now, Lindsay.' All the members roared.

With a mixture of splendid defence, two cracking boundaries, and the patience of Job, Kline defied all the West Indians could throw at him and his senior partner, the indefatigable Ken 'Slasher' Mackay. They faced a considerable bowling line-up, led by the explosive fast man Wes Hall, who seemingly pushed off from the sightscreen for every delivery (which was a very long way in Adelaide in those days), the game's greatest all-rounder Garry Sobers, medium-pacer Frank Worrell and spinners Lance Gibbs and Alf Valentine. The Windies attack bowled 120 eight-ball overs in the Australian second innings.

But they failed to break that last pair. All Australia seemed glued to the radio broadcast. Spinner's wife, Stella, with three-year-old Elizabeth and eight-week-old Susan, was listening to the exciting last moments of the match with Colin McDonald's wife, Lois, in their home in bayside Beaumaris, Melbourne.

In Brisbane in the first Test Kline had endured the agony of facing up in the last over when one run was needed for victory. This time Mackay had to survive the last ball to avoid defeat. A rising delivery from Hall struck him fair on the chest. He had let the ball hit him rather than risk getting an edge.

Spinner Kline scored his highest Test score that day, 15 not out. More importantly he endured for 104 minutes, even though he hadn't been able to lay bat on ball in the nets. As things turned out, it was the last time he was to play Test cricket. It's a strange thing, but his 15 not out is the thing he is best remembered for, not the hat-trick he took against South Africa at Cape Town in 1957–58, nor any other of the 34 wickets he took in his 13 Tests.

The partnership between Kline and Meckiff in Brisbane lasted but one ball; their partnership off the field spanned decades. The two have been regulars for many years at the scene of Kline's memorable innings, the Adelaide Test. For more than 40 years the pair have been great friends with former SA and Test wicketkeeper Barry 'BJ' Jarman. At least once a year over many years they'd drive to Adelaide and hook up with Norm O'Neill for a rollicking few days on board Jarman's houseboat, *Goodas Gold*, on the Murray River.

One night as BJ, Norm and Meckiff spun stories over a convivial red wine or two, Spinner excused himself.

Time went by and Meckiff quipped: 'Where's Spinner? He's probably fallen in.'

At a secluded spot on the river, ropes secured the boat to a couple of trees. There was a plank from the back of the boat to the sandy shore. Meckiff was right: they found Spinner hanging on to the side of the boat, saturated and laughing his head off.

Next day Spinner announced that he had lost his glasses. Two days later they returned to that mooring spot and there were Spinner's glasses, murky water washing over them on the shore line.

Jarman and co. would often scold him on the houseboat trips over that innings in Adelaide. 'How come you scored only 15 in a whole session? Terrible batting, Spinner.'

In 1961 during his England tour with Australia, the side played a couple of one-day matches in Ireland. In Belfast the wind blew to near-hurricane force, but Richie Benaud was determined to lead his side onto the ground. Benaud, however, wasn't keen to bowl into the wind that wild Irish day. He left that task to Spinner Kline.

Spinner was a slow left-armer, twirling the ball down after his jaunty little run-up that culminated in a brilliant kangaroo hop just before he hit the crease.

'Spinner wasn't the quickest through the air and not only couldn't he get the ball up, I doubted whether it would reach the other end,' Jarman recalled of that Irish match.

Spinner loved a good red and watching the television show *Judge Judy*.

In the last year of his life, he was greatly buoyed by the golfing prowess of his granddaughter, 17-year-old Olivia Kline, who in January 2015 won the SA Junior Masters by a whopping nine strokes at Royal Adelaide Gold Club. Spinner – a lovely bloke. A legend, a little champ.

JOHNNY MARTIN

'The Favourite'

They called him 'The Favourite' and he proved as entertaining
a cricketer as Australian cricket ever produced. As a down the
list batsman Johnny hit out from the outset and his bowling was
a throwback to the days of Chuck Fleetwood-Smith, a left-arm
Chinaman merchant.

Born in Wingham on 28 July 1931, John Wesley Martin spent his
formative years on the NSW Central Coast near Taree. He was one
of 10 children. His father managed the Burrell Creek Post Office
and general store, and in later years Johnny took over the role from
his dad. Johnny's mother was related to the Tom Richardson who
bowled so valiantly for Surrey and England in the 1890s.

Martin first went down to Sydney at the age of 15 to watch an
Ashes Test at the SCG. He saw Don Bradman and Sid Barnes carve
up the England attack, each scoring 234 in that summer of 1946–47.
The chirpy little all-rounder's imagination was fired and he yearned
to one day play on the mighty SCG. From that day on Johnny's cricket
strategy was sealed: spin hard and hit out at every opportunity.

In 1953–54 Martin's reputation in the bush was such that he received an offer to join the Petersham Cricket Club in Sydney. He caught the train from Burrell Creek, played the match at a Sydney suburban ground on the Saturday and returned home by train after the day's play.

Teammates and opposition players alike loved Johnny's passion for the game. Spectators loved his attacking attitude. Here was a spinner who spun hard. His appeals were sometimes almost gentle and on other occasions a loud demand to be answered in the affirmative by the umpire. He never made any fuss when an appeal was turned down, just bustled back to his mark for the next ball. His batting was all vigour. Johnny hit some 166 sixes for Petersham in grade cricket.

Eventually picked for the NSW state team in the season of 1956–57, Martin played for NSW until the summer of 1967–68. He did have one season for South Australia in 1958–59 and took 7/110 against Peter May's Englishmen on the Adelaide Oval without winning Test selection. Martin had a couple of tours to New Zealand, one with a young Australian team in 1956–57 and another under Ian Craig three years later, although in those days Australia did not afford New Zealand Test match status.

Martin played three Tests in the exciting series against the touring West Indians in 1960–61, including fielding (as a substitute) in the Tied Test at the Gabba.

He debuted in the third Test at the MCG, hitting out grandly for 55 in a 97-run partnership with Ken Mackay, which extended Australia's total to 348, enough to bring about a seven-wicket victory. In the West Indian second innings Martin dismissed three luminaries – Rohan Kanhai, Garry Sobers and Frank Worrell. Kanhai fell to a mistimed pull; Sobers was lured forward to a curving, dipping leg break and was caught by Bobby Simpson at first slip, and Worrell was also caught by Simpson for a duck to complete a 'pair' for the match.

In 1961 Johnny had a season with Colne in the Lancashire League, taking 70 wickets at an average of 12 and belting 700-odd runs at 35.

'Little Fav' seemed to be everyone's favourite. He didn't play much Test cricket but on the domestic scene the happy little bloke with a bouncy disposition kept getting wickets for NSW. In 1962–63 he took a career best 8/97 against Victoria in Sydney and the next summer he scored his only first-class century (101), against WA in Perth. That summer of 1963–64 he played one Test, against South Africa at the MCG, taking four wickets. He toured England with Bobby Simpson's Australian side in 1964 but because of trouble with his bowling shoulder didn't get a Test.

On the way home he played two Tests – one in India and one in Pakistan. All up he took eight wickets. His was pretty much one or two Tests on, and many a Test off. It must have been difficult for him for he could not build any sort of momentum or continuity. Martin toured South Africa in 1966–67, but played just one Test, his last, at Port Elizabeth, where he went wicketless.

The much-loved Martin scored 214 runs in eight Tests at 17.83 with a top score of 55. He took 17 Test wickets at 48.94 and in all first-class matches captured 445 wickets at 31.17. The Favourite never set the world alight in Test cricket, but he brought a warmth to the game that made him a favourite of fellow players, press and public.

DAVID SINCOCK

He made the ball sing

David Sincock was arguably the spinner who got more purchase on the ball than any other. That is saying something, for Shane Warne sure made the ball hum, so much spin did he impart on the ball. Spin, of course, is not everything – Warne had tremendous control, whereas with Sincock often the ball fell way too short or was lobbed like a hand grenade at head height. He was fortunate indeed that he had Les Favell as his state captain, for Favell didn't mind a bowler going for runs so long as he took wickets at regular intervals.

A left-arm Chinaman bowler, Sincock hailed from the Glenelg Cricket Club, the home of the Chappell brothers. At the age of 16 in the summer of 1960–61 he demolished a strong NSW side on the Adelaide Oval in a sensational debut, talking 6/52. The NSW side boasted such greats as Neil Harvey, Norm O'Neill, Richie Benaud and Alan Davidson. His performance was at the end of the 1960–61 season, just a month or two before the Australians toured England. One wonders what might have been for Sincock had he made that tour under the guidance of Benaud instead of having to bide his time for a Test chance after Benaud had retired. When he landed the ball it was like a bomb about to explode. Good judges reckon Sincock could make a ball turn on a sheet of ice. They nicknamed Sincock 'Evil', and when he landed the ball in a good area it was pure magic.

He made his Test debut against Pakistan at the MCG in December 1964. In 1965 he played another against the West Indies in Port of Spain, then finally one more against England at the SCG in 1966. Those three Tests yielded Sincock eight wickets at 51.25 In 46 first-class matches he took 159 wickets at 36.87.

Statistics never tell the full story. I have in my mind's eye the sight of Evil, wrist cocked as he came in to bowl with energy and purpose and the ball fairly buzzing down the track. Evil Sincock made the ball sing.

TOM VEIVERS

The economical one

When Tom Veivers stepped out on to the Gabba in late 1963 he was the first genuine conventional off-break bowler to play for Australia since Ian Johnson had retired seven years earlier. A hard-working all-rounder, Veivers bowled right-arm and batted left-handed. As with Johnny Martin, Veivers loved hitting the ball and often lifted it clear over the fence. He didn't spin much, but was accurate and ground away to build pressure from his end, helping the more attacking bowlers at the other end grab the glory.

Veivers played 21 Test matches, scoring 813 runs at 31.26 and took just 33 wickets at 41.66 with a best of 4/68. He came into the game near the end of the Benaud era and toured England with the Australian team in 1964 under the captaincy of Bob Simpson. In the Old Trafford Test Veivers bowled one of the longest spells in Test history, wheeling down 95.1 six-ball overs, with 36 maidens, for a return of 3/155. It remains the highest number of balls bowled in an innings of a Test match by an Australian. His last tour was to South Africa in 1966–67 and he retired from first-class cricket the following year. A jolly, likeable chap, Veivers became a Brisbane radio station executive before serving as secretary of the Queensland Cricket Association from 1974 to 1977. In addition he was a Queensland state selector from 1977 to 1982. From 1983 to 1986 Veivers had a brief political career, holding the seat of Ashgrove for the ALP in the Legislative Assembly of Queensland. His cousins Mick and Greg Veivers both played rugby league for Australia and his great nephew Jack Wildermuth has played T20 Internationals for Australia. Tom Veivers will be fondly remembered as a hard-hitting all-rounder with a pleasant disposition and a good team man.

His marathon bowling stint at Old Trafford in 1964 is his lasting legacy.

TONY LOCK

The spinner who gave the West belief

It is the summer of 1967–68 and the great England spinner Tony Lock is toiling away on the Adelaide Oval. Sir Donald Bradman sidles up to Ian McLachlan, then a recently retired SA batsman and later a Liberal MP and the driving force behind the $500 million Adelaide Oval re-build.

'This fella Lock is the best left-arm spinner I've seen since Hedley Verity.'

Verity was the England spinner who excelled between the wars. He captured Bradman's wicket 10 times, so he must have been some bowler.

Lock hailed from Surrey and formed the famous spin partnership with off spinner Jim Laker. The Surrey spin twins were also the England spin twins in the 1950s. When Laker took those 19 wickets against Australia at Old Trafford in 1956, it was Lock who took the remaining wicket at the other end.

Graham Anthony Richard Lock was born in Limpsfield, Surrey, on Friday 5 July 1929. Thanks to the substantial influence of

Sir HDG Leveson Gower, a stockbroker and cricket power broker with Surrey and the MCC, the 17-year-old Lock was thrust into first-class cricket on 13 July 1946.

Lock did not play regularly for Surrey until 1949. Two years later he bagged 105 wickets for his county – and he broke the 100-wicket barrier every year up to and including 1962. Twice he took in excess of 200 wickets for the season. He made his Test debut, against India, in 1952, and came of age with sterling performances in the fourth and fifth Tests against Lindsay Hassett's Australians in 1953. He, along with spin twin Jim Laker, spun the Aussies to their doom at The Oval where England regained the Ashes. He was named as one of the Five Cricketers of the Year in the 1954 edition of *Wisden Cricketers' Almanack*. However, Lock had to withstand lots of accusations that he threw the occasional delivery. In 1958 Lock destroyed New Zealand with 34 wickets in their series at the astonishing average of 7.47. After failing badly on the 1958–59 Australian tour, England played a few Tests in New Zealand, where he took 13 wickets at an average under nine runs apiece. It was on this tour that he was shown footage of his bowling – and that film shocked him into remodelling his action.

By 1961 he was back in the England side against Richie Benaud's visiting Australian team. He was dropped for the 1962–63 Ashes series in Australia, but he had already taken up an offer to play for Western Australia.

The aggressive Lock made an immediate and lasting impact on WA. As captain of the state team he toiled manfully with the ball, hit some runs down the order and caught anything within cooee.

He had the surest hands I've seen of any spin bowler. No matter how hard a batsman hit a catch his way, he plucked the ball as though he were plucking a cherry to beat a marauding bird swooping in for a meal. When the fast bowlers were operating Lock stationed himself at leg slip or a squarer position at short backward leg. He made the impossible look easy. For WA against the visiting England team he caught Colin Cowdrey at leg slip. Before the Kipper had time to turn about Lock had pocketed the ball.

The WA Cricket Association had Lock coach a group of emerging spinners, among them Terry Jenner, Tony Mann, John Inverarity and me. We could see at close range the brilliance of Lock's bowling. He seemed to have the ball on a string, such was his control of flight and the subtle changes of pace that had the batsmen ever floundering. I batted against him for Mt Lawley in a grade match. He had me wavering all over the place before he bowled me behind my legs. I think I was watching him, mesmerised, like a rabbit caught in the spotlight, and not doing what I was supposed to be doing; yes, watching the ball. One day during one of Lockie's coaching lessons he suggested I change my grip. I used to hold the ball with the index and third finger widely spaced, along the seam, not across the seam as he advocated.

I tried to explain that I was only following the advice of an author named Christopher Sly, who wrote *How to Bowl Them Out*, where the illustration for an off-break had the fingers widely spaced along the seam.

'Never heard of him, mate,' Lock said. 'Think about it. If your fingers are widely spaced across the seam you will easily achieve hitting the turf right on the seam, 99 per cent of the time.' It took me a while to adjust and he was dead right.

Lock moved back to England every Australian winter. In 1965 he joined Leicestershire and was made captain for the following two seasons. In 1967 he took the club to second place in the County Championship.

In the summer of 1966–67 I was selected in the WA state team as 12th man for two matches. Lock was the old pro and he insisted that I brew up a pot of tea in the very pot he used to bring with him to the match. 'None of this tea-bag stuff, Ash. Proper tea leaves ... and let the tea brew ... no cat's piss.'

Outstanding WA all-rounder Ian Brayshaw remembers his first impression of Lock.

> He was much bigger – taller and stronger in build than I expected. And there was this unmistakeable Londoner accent, delivered in a croaky voice. Tony was farmed out to my club, Claremont-Cottesloe, whom I had led the previous season. I happily agreed to stand aside.
>
> Before our first meeting with the players, he asked to speak to me outside. Then he said in a more refined voice, 'Ian, you can call me Tony ... but I want the others to call me Mr Lock or Skipper.' That lasted about one second with the lads.
>
> The essence of his greatness for WA was his deadly control of line, length, plus his variations of pace and flight. He would find those variations through changing his position on the crease and, sometimes, sending one down from as far as two metres behind the crease. He rarely bowled in the nets. But you could bet your house that his first ball out in the middle would be perfect in line and length.

Brayshaw recalls Lock one day unleashing a blindingly fast ball to clean bowl Norm O'Neill at the WACA ground. Coincidentally I was on the ground as 12th man in a straight fielding position, I suspect deep and straight at mid-off. O'Neill smashed the first seven balls of Lock's over straight to me. The last ball was quick, very quick, and it curved in late. O'Neill was done by pace and the swerve. He ended up falling headlong and bracing himself with both hands to the side of the wicket as the ball crashed into the stumps.

Up until that Lock 'special' O'Neill was completely in control, eyeing a century at 70 not out. Funny thing, in the second dig Normie was again on the rampage and I was called on to field at deep, straight mid-off. First seven balls same deal: all of them blasted along the ground to me. Last ball of the over and Lock unleashed his quicker one. That too crashed into O'Neill's stumps. Over a beer in the dressing-room Normie walked up to Tony and said, 'Hey Lockie, that was a chuck today and it was a chuck the other day.'

'Norm, what can I say? I think you are right on both counts.'

As Brayshaw and others would attest, Lock was an inspirational leader.

'He was a "do as I do" skipper, just what our young WA side needed. He taught us how to play winning cricket – a priceless lesson. It was up to other leaders, John Inverarity and Rod Marsh at that time, to teach us how to keep winning.'

Brayshaw described Lock as the 'complete pro'.

He bound his knees up in bandages and gave his all – which was a mountainous contribution to the team. Diving around the field, though not necessarily chasing too hard, finding the energy to bowl long spells and contributing to a much younger team's camaraderie both in the dressing-room and on the road.

Lock's Test career began in 1952 and ended in 1968. In that time he played 49 Tests, taking 174 wickets at 25.58. In all first-class matches he took 2844 wickets at 19.23.

As a batsman he scored 742 runs in Tests at 13.59, with a top score of 59, and in all first-class matches he scored 10,342 runs at 15.88 with a top score of 89.

In the Sheffield Shield competition for WA, Lock played 66 matches taking 302 wickets at 23.87.

His influence on Australian cricket and WA specifically was immense. Lock's influence on spin bowling Down Under and the spinners who emerged during his time with WA was invaluable.

Tony Lock was an amazing cricketer. Seeing him bowl and weave a net about a batsman was like watching a spider and a fly. He had the ability to trap the batsman ball by ball, then end his agony with that fatal delivery. Lock got many top-order players out over his long career, but it was how he set up the tailender and finally finished him off that was so entertaining. He could catch a cricket ball going at breakneck speed; high or low, it mattered not. His hands were magnificent and even better off his own bowling. He began with a shock of red hair, but it receded early and in no time he resembled a trimmer version of Friar Tuck. Lock taught us in WA how to win consistently.

Former WA captain, Test batsman and deputy to Lock John Inverarity said:

I played with Tony Lock for Western Australia for nine seasons, 1962–63 to 1970–71 inclusive. During that period Tony had enormous success as a slow left-hand orthodox bowler. He was not one to put a lot of revs on the ball, but he had unerring accuracy, subtle changes of pace, nerve, competitive edge and an instinctive shrewd ability to use his repertoire to his advantage. I often think you can judge a bowler on two criteria, the first being sheer talent – pace, swing, turn, drop, control. The other relates to hunting instinct and presence. When exactly to bowl a bouncer, or a yorker, or toss one high, or wide, or squeeze the life out of a struggling batsman with accuracy and a measure of theatre.

I would score Dennis Lillee, Malcolm Marshall, Wasim Akram, Shane Warne and some others ten out of ten on both criteria. I would allocate ten to Tony Lock on the second of these criteria, but not on the first, though high.

The young WA spinners who learnt so much under Lock's tutelage are eternally grateful. To have one-on-one sessions with one of the great left-arm spinners in the world was brilliant. He would spend about an hour or more chatting to the youngsters, then he'd pick up a ball and with a few little skips to the crease would bowl a hard-spun, dipping delivery right on a perfect length.

Australian cricket generally and WA cricket specifically owes Tony Lock a great deal.

Tony Lock (centre) with me, Ashley Mallett (left), and Garry Sobers, the greatest all-rounder in history. (ASHLEY MALLETT COLLECTION)

THE
INTERREGNUM

When Richie Benaud retired Australia wondered just when the next top-flight spinner might emerge. As in the Old Mother Hubbard fairytale, the cupboard was bare. Within a few years Johnny Martin, Tom Veivers and Peter Philpott had either hung up their boots or were on the verge of doing so. It got to the stage on the tour of South Africa in 1966–67 that much of the spin-bowling duties rested on the shoulders of captain Bobby Simpson and part-time leggies Ian Chappell and Keith Stackpole.

By the late 1960s Victorian batsman and off spinner Bob Cowper was still wheeling away, and on the Australian tour of England in 1968 he put in some splendid efforts. Another more than useful exponent of the spinning art was WA batsman John Inverarity. He took 221 first-class wickets at 30.67 in 223 matches. In his six Tests he took a total of 4/93 including 3/26 off 33 overs on the Fusarium wicket – named after the fungus that ruined the pitch – that was Headingly, Leeds, in 1972. No doubt Inverarity learnt much from the great left-arm spinner Tony Lock. Another useful performer was the left-arm wrist spinner from NSW David 'Cracka' Hourn, who took 164 wickets in just 44 first-class matches at 28.71, with 11 hauls of five wickets and two of 10 in a game. Although Hourn was a splendid bowler of the Chinaman variety, his eyesight was so bad his fielding was sub-standard and his batting even worse; it precluded him from any Australian team.

He wore thick glasses – 'Coke bottles glasses' we called them – and once when bowling at the SCG his glasses fell to the pitch in his follow-through. South African great Barry Richards was at the non-striker's end, playing for South Australia. He saw the chance for a bit of mischief, and nudged the glasses away from Cracka, who ended up on his knees before his searching hands finally nailed the all-important eyewear. It was a pity, because Cracka could have been a sensation in Test cricket, especially on the soft, responsive tracks of England and New Zealand.

By the late 1960s a new lot of spinners of genuine Test match potential emerged, among them Johnny 'Cho' Gleeson, the NSW finger-flick spinner; leg spinner Kerry O'Keeffe; yours truly and Terry Jenner, both from South Australia; WA's leg spinner Tony Mann; Victoria's leg spinner Jim Higgs; left-arm orthodox spinner Ray Bright; Queensland and WA leg spinner Bob Paulsen; WA off spinner Bruce 'Roo' Yardley; and Queensland leg spinners Trevor Hohns and Malcolm Francke. All had their days in the sun, except Francke. Born in Sri Lanka, the leg spinner played for Queensland but never a Test for Australia. I always thought that he should have done so for he was, to my mind, among the best of the leggies going around in this era.

A little further down the track came NSW off spinner and splendid batsman Greg 'Mo' Matthews, NSW leggie Bob 'Dutchy' Holland and left-armer Murray Bennett; WA left-arm orthodox spinner Tom Hogan; SA off spinner Tim May, who really came of age a few years later, forming a great spin partnership for a while with Shane Warne, and SA leg-spinning all-rounder Peter 'Sounda' Sleep, who excelled as an all-rounder in first-class cricket for SA, but struggled for consistency on the Test stage. In 14 Tests he hit 483 runs at 24.15 and took 31 wickets at 45.06.

Champion batsman Allan Border also bowled more than handy left-arm orthodox spinners, once taking 11 wickets in a match against Clive Lloyd's West Indians on the SCG. It was a nasty, dusty turner and the West Indies went into the match without a spinner, dependent as usual on their barrage of pacemen. But AB outdid them all, with some good balls and some long hops, taking four wickets in one innings and 7/46 in the other. NSW off spinner Peter Taylor bowled some good off spin around this time, once getting 6/78 against England, but he really didn't kick on.

One of the greatest problems for cricketers in this era, perhaps more than in any other, was to hold down a job while pursuing international cricket. Even post-Packer the money was insufficient. Previously employers such as the Commonwealth Bank and cigarette companies allowed their Test men time off on full pay, but not so much anymore.

When Dennis Lillee was joined by the whirlwind fast bowler Jeff Thomson at the start of the 1974–75 summer, pace bowling left spin bowling for dead. I took my 100th Test wicket in my 23rd Test – and then just 32 wickets in my final 15 Tests. When Australia beat the West Indies 5–1 in the summer of 1975–76, captain Clive Lloyd was convinced that a barrage of pace was the way to go – and boy did the Windies run roughshod over world cricket for years. There was no respite from the likes of Andy Roberts, Michael Holding, Malcolm Marshall, Joel Garner, Colin Croft and so many others. They couldn't fit them all into the one Test team, but four of them invariably did and batting against this constant pace barrage was akin to Bodyline Revisited.

While pace ruled the Test match stage, spinners hardly got a look in. If they did, and I did, it was to play a bit part. To survive you had to get a few runs down the list and field out of your skin.

JOHN GLEESON

Groucho Marx meets Ronnie Corbett

The dictum commonly attributed to Abraham Lincoln proved true in the case of John Gleeson, for he fooled all of the batsmen some of the time. Yes, for a time in the late 1960s and in the early 1970s some of the world's most accomplished batsmen were perplexed, bemused and frustrated when trying to pick the direction of spin by this slim little bloke from the NSW country town of Tamworth. That's the Australian home of country music, but Gleeson never sang anything like a poetic Song of Spin. In my mind's eye, I can see 'Cho' now. He moves in with a funny gait, a bit like a comical mix of Groucho Marx and Ronnie Corbett. He's not a short man, and stays low. The delivery doesn't make a fizzing sound at all; it glides out of that folded-finger grip, always on target, but devoid of loop or shape.

Gleeson was a man of principle, and never resorted to sledging. In 1969–70 he was one of those who, led by skipper Bill Lawry, spoke up against the Australian administrators' desire to milk another Test out of a team frazzled by the stresses and strains of a 4–0 shellacking in South Africa, straight after five Tests in India.

He had two main deliveries: a flat trajectory off-break and a leg break with a seeming off-break action. Sometimes he tried to fool the batsman with a seam-up straight one, but he only bowled that one when all else failed him. That he could cause so much disharmony among batsmen had some cricketers, including me, stumped, for he was easy as pie to pick. If only I had batted as well as those who couldn't pick him.

Gleeson was Australia's second-most accomplished finger-flick spinner, but not in the same class as Jack Iverson of the 1950s. Indeed Iverson's unique style inspired Gleeson. At the age of 12 Johnny read about the finger-flick bowler in a magazine article.

Iverson was an inspiration to many, a 'Mr Magic' with the ability to make a seeming off-break turn from the leg and what appeared to be a leg break come back into the right-hander. His finger-flicking mystery bowling style immediately held great fascination for young Gleeson, whose long, slender fingers were ideal for spinning a ball, and especially well-suited to the folded finger grip used by Iverson.

Gleeson began his cricketing life as a wicketkeeper and when he moved from Tamworth to Sydney with the Postmaster-General's Department in 1956 he kept in the lower grades for Western Suburbs. He discovered that he could confound batsmen with one particular delivery. He held the ball with his folded third finger across the seam.

Gleeson would cut down the right side and the action looked for all the world like an off-break or an off-cutter. Then, as his right arm came over, his folded third finger came into play. He flicked it to the left. So cutting down to the right then flicking to the left had batsmen confused and struggling to detect which way the ball was going. I can do it with a ping pong ball, but you need exceptionally strong fingers to bowl this way with a hard cricket ball.

He trained alone in secret, trying to master the finger-flick bowling.

In 1958, at the age of 20, Gleeson returned to Tamworth. He won selection for an overseas tour of Canada with The Emu Club, a travelling social cricket club in those years. Frustrated that his bowlers couldn't make inroads in the opposition batting, Gleeson shed the pads and first began to bowl his 'Iverson' style.

He first bowled in a serious match in Melbourne in 1964, turning out for the Australian Postal Institute. His captain was Tom Brooks, former NSW fast bowler and Test umpire. His deliveries mystified all and sundry that day, many deliveries beating the bat and the wicketkeeper. By the summer of 1965–66 Gleeson was the first-choice spinner for Gunnedah. Jack Chegwyn, a great promoter of country cricket in NSW, took sides festooned with current and former Test cricketers to the outlying areas, ever on the lookout for raw talent.

Gleeson took wickets in the match and delighted in getting the chance to bowl to Richie Benaud, one of his boyhood heroes.

Benaud knew exciting talent when he saw it and he took a big interest in Gleeson, recommending him to the Balmain Club, which had as its secretary Fred Bennett, who was destined to one day become chairman of the Australian Cricket Board.

Gleeson got bags of wickets for Balmain and in 1966–67 he made his debut for NSW at the WACA ground in Perth. He bowled 23 overs into the wind, the Fremantle Doctor, but Gleeson found operating on the hard, true surface at the WACA less than ideal. He took one wicket and was made to carry the drinks in the next match in Adelaide.

Being 12th man in Australian cricket in those days meant four days of drudgery. You sat about when the team fielded and sometimes got on the field, but usually it was carrying the drinks and attending to the players' every whim. And some players treated the 12th man poorly. However, Gleeson's first stint as 12th man in Adelaide proved a godsend.

Sir Donald Bradman, then chairman of the Test selectors, met NSW captain Brian Booth on the eve of the match and asked him who was going to be 12th man.

'Johnny Gleeson,' Booth said confidently.

'Well, that's the first mistake you've made this game.'

Bradman always made it his business to know all about emerging players. He well remembered how Iverson had bamboozled Freddie Brown's Englishmen and he wondered whether this bloke Gleeson could do a similar job on Ray Illingworth's team down the track. When NSW batted, Sir Donald asked Gleeson if he would like to accompany him to the nets and bowl to him.

Bradman was then aged 58. He wore neither pads nor gloves, but half a dozen balls from Gleeson was enough for him to say, 'Thanks, John. By the end of the season I think you'll be playing for Australia.'

Gleeson toured New Zealand with an Australian Second XI in 1967 and by December of the same year he had made his Test debut against India. He played in all four Tests, taking the last three wickets in the third Test to help Australia win by 39 runs.

Gleeson was a certain selection for England in 1968. He was dubbed 'Cho' for 'Cricket Hours Only' – once play was done, Gleeson was gone. Maybe he wanted to maintain the mystery.

Cho revelled in the mystery. He was very much the man of the moment. Upon our arrival at the Waldorf Hotel, our London home away from home, there was Lawry talking about playing bright cricket ('so long as we win') and Cho fast asleep in the background, his head resting on 'Garth' McKenzie's broad right shoulder.

I roomed with Cho in 1968 and one day asked how the publicity affected him.

'Doesn't worry me in the slightest,' he said. 'Never read the newspapers.'

Next I found him trying to close the lid on a suitcase filled to overflowing with newspaper cuttings of one mystery finger-flick bowler, John Gleeson. He had the dry, quirky sense of humour of the Outback Australia of long ago.

By 1968 Bill Lawry had taken over from Bob Simpson as Test captain. Lawry liked to keep runs at bay. He managed his fast- and medium-paced attack brilliantly; but when it came to spin, Lawry could play it well, but he didn't understand spinners.

However, Lawry did like the way Gleeson bowled. Cho operated with a flat trajectory and was more at home on a green-top than a slow, dusty turner, thus complementing the likes of the fast men Graham McKenzie, Alan Connolly, Neil Hawke and their ilk.

Cho didn't set the world on fire in India in 1969. Apart from the Bombay Test, where the wicket had bounce and pace, Gleeson struggled to make an impact.

But he did make an impact of a different sort on the last day of our match against South Zone at Bangalore.

Set 200 runs to get in two hours and 50 minutes, we collapsed to the masterly spin of Erapalli Prasanna, who by the fall of our sixth wicket had the incredible figures of 6/9 off nine overs. Barnacle Bill Lawry was battling out for a draw at the other end when Cho strolled to the wicket with the air of a man without a care in the world.

He sauntered to square leg whereupon he spoke quietly to umpire BN Nagaraj before heading straight down the wicket to chat to the official at Prasanna's end, umpire NS Rishi.

That done, Cho leaned over his bat, rejecting the umpire's request to take guard, quipping, 'Not required, Mr Umpire. I took guard in Bombay weeks ago.'

While Lawry defended stoically, Gleeson either padded away or hit out.

Stumps were drawn five minutes before the scheduled close because a section of the crowd began throwing stones.

Lawry batted for all 52 overs for an unconquered 10, Cho was not out 18 and Australia at stumps was 8/90.

There were back slaps all round for Barnacle Bill and Cho, but Ian Chappell, Doug Walters and co. were far more interested in what Cho said to the umpires.

'Well I said to the ump at square leg: "Mr Umpire if you give me out LBW I will wrap this bat about your head" – and I said the same thing to the other umpire.'

Probably his crowning glory was his Test bowling against South Africa in 1970.

The South Africans had a powerful batting line-up, headed by Graeme Pollock, Barry Richards, Eddie Barlow and Mike Procter. Only Richards could play Gleeson effectively.

When asked by others, including his teammates, Richards would say: 'If you go after it and hit the ball just as it lands it matters not which way the ball turns.'

Barlow tried that very thing against Cho in the third Test at Johannesburg, didn't quite get to the pitch of the ball and Brian Taber politely whipped off the bails with the man they called 'Bunter' yards out of his ground.

In the four Tests Gleeson bowled 255 overs against the South Africans, taking 19 wickets at 38.94. He bowled a good deal better than his figures reflect.

Cho's bowling mystified many a good batsman and Ray Illingworth's 1970–71 Ashes squad was no exception.

In the SCG fourth Test John Edrich waltzed up the pitch for a mid-wicket chat with his opening partner, Geoff Boycott.

'Hey Boycs,' Edrich said joyfully, 'I've just worked out Gleeson. I know for sure where each one's going.'

'Oh, is that all, Eddie,' Boycott laughed. 'I worked Cho out two Tests ago … but don't tell those other boogers in the dressing-room.'

John Gleeson was a great character. He spoke with passion about bowling, especially spin bowling, and the mystery of the finger-flicking style.

One who was bamboozled was WA all-rounder Ian Brayshaw, who was having trouble picking Gleeson while batting with Rod Marsh at the SCG.

> I survived by thrusting my front pad way forward and getting bat on the one going leg to off, taking the other one on the pad. I recall Cho didn't have that much patience, because he was bound to throw in a fully or half-tracker most overs, so I could make a few runs! At the end of an over, sensing the bleeding obvious, Bacchus came up to me and the conversation went something like this:
>
> 'You're not picking him, are you?'
>
> Pause.
>
> 'No.'
>
> 'Would you like some help?'
>
> Pause.
>
> 'Well ...'
>
> 'I can tell which one he's going to bowl from the way he puts the ball in his hand ... would you like me to give you a signal?

Brayshaw's reply is best left unprinted.

Ah, another psychological win for the 'man of mystery'.

Just as he loved the Iverson way, Cho later delighted in the similar finger-flicking style of Sri Lanka's Ajantha Mendis. He proved to us all that some wicketkeepers can turn their hand successfully to spin bowling. Cho certainly turned heads with his style. And to have the then chairman of Australia's Test selectors Sir Donald Don Bradman in your corner was quite something.

Johnny Gleeson played 29 Tests taking 93 wickets at 36.20. His best series performance was 30 wickets against the West Indies in Australia in 1968–69. His tight and economical bowling suited skipper Bill Lawry, but before Dennis Lillee burst onto the scene

Australia needed wickets from their leading spinner up the other end, for the pace bowlers at the time were near the end of their careers. The great speedster Graham McKenzie was a shadow of his former self, so too Alan Connolly.

In 116 first-class matches Gleeson took 430 wickets at 24.95.

His efforts probably didn't match what Bradman had envisioned for him, but for a former wicketkeeper who taught himself a new skill, Cho did himself and his nation proud, proving that there is a certain magic to be found for those who seek a different path to success.

KERRY O'KEEFFE

'Watch that man Mark Burgess!'

When Kerry O'Keeffe burst onto the first-class scene in the late 1960s there was a lather of excitement among the press, especially in NSW. The youngster bowled leg spinners at a brisk pace, which alone was reason enough for him to be unfairly likened to the great Bill O'Reilly. O'Keeffe performed well for NSW from the outset and his tight leg spinners were complemented by solid batting and safe fielding, usually in the gully or backward point. However, when he was being touted to play Test cricket, he became weighed down mentally by expectations that he would be the new star spinner of the 1970s – and it showed. He seemed to change his action from one summer to the next trying to find that perfect repeatable action that spinners seek but rarely find. For some obscure reason Kerry was nicknamed 'Skull' and the sobriquet stuck fast.

Skull it was and Skull it is. During his cricket career he was always deadly serious; he could laugh, but not at himself.

After 24 Tests and retirement from first-class cricket, Skull eventually found his niche in broadcasting, especially for the ABC, dragging that rather dull cricket broadcaster into the 21st century with a madcap mix of jokes (usually nothing related to the cricket at hand), and a hysterical laugh that had the happy knack of getting his fellow commentators and audience to laugh along with him. His on-air partnership with visiting Indian commentator Harsha Bhogle was particularly entertaining. His joke about a frog, whose father was Mick Jagger, applying for a bank loan is one people still recount and retell.

Yet Skull didn't always find things so funny with his teammates in the Australian team. During the 1974 Australian tour of New Zealand we played Auckland in Auckland. Skull was 80-odd not out when the Australian No 11 came in. Skull had never scored a first-class hundred, although he did hit a Test 85 against NZ in Adelaide a few months earlier and a few years later would open the batting for Australia in the second innings of the Centenary Test, when Rick McCosker was nursing a broken jaw.

I sidled up to Skull and said, 'Mate, I will be here for you at the end. They won't get me out.' What a confidence boost that must have been for him. Auckland had a couple of Test bowlers: the indefatigable fast-medium merchant Bob Cunis and left-arm orthodox spinner Hedley Howarth. They also had a brilliant fieldsman in Mark Burgess.

Now, for any batsman, Burgess in the field was a man to watch very carefully. He was lightning fast across the turf and he had a deadly accurate, bullet-like throw.

Skull was batting well, playing strokes to all parts of the field. He was on track to score that maiden first-class century. I kept saying: 'I'll be there at the end, Skull. Stay with me.'

Steadily Skull's score mounted.

At times off the last ball of an over I sacrificed a single so Skull kept strike. He cracked Cunis beautifully through the covers to the fence, bringing himself to within one run of those magical three figures.

O'Keeffe, 99 not out.

There were four balls of the over to go.

A mid-wicket conference ensued.

'Nothing silly … no run-outs, Rowdy.'

'Now Skull, this is vital,' I warned him. 'Watch that man Mark Burgess lurking at cover point. He's dynamite. Whatever you do, DON'T run if it goes anywhere near Burgess.'

The very next Cunis delivery saw Skull push the ball a foot to the left of Burgess and charge down the wicket for his 100th run.

For a moment I hesitated – didn't Skull listen to anything I said? – before scampering towards the other end. From the corner of my eye I could see Burgess swoop. I assumed that Skull made his ground easily for I caught a glimpse of a red leather sphere heading straight towards the wicketkeeper's end … the very end I needed to make good my ground.

I dived and slid in a cloud of dust, but to my horror my bat stuck fast in the Eden Park dust. As I lay on my side at least one metre from home I watched the bails being whipped off by the wicketkeeper, RA Dykes.

And there was Red Ink O'Keeffe at the other end. He had reached his ground easily and stood there unconquered on 99. We made our way back to the Australian dressing-room, where deathly silence reigned. I scanned the faces and the blokes' eyes seemed to dance excitedly. Then Rod Marsh and Doug Walters burst out laughing. So did I. Skull didn't.

Skull didn't laugh at all. Not on your Nelly. He was fuming. Probably still is, although I suspect he will bring more laughter to others with his version of events that day in Auckland.

Whenever we catch up I can't resist asking Skull, 'What's your highest first-class score?' Still, 99 not out isn't too bad for a highest score on the CV of a cricketer who was primarily a bowler.

The 24 Tests that Skull played, starting at the MCG against England in January 1971 and ending against the same opposition at Trent Bridge in 1977, brought him 53 wickets at an average of 38.07. With the bat he scored 644 at 25.76 – and of course never scored a Test hundred. Remarkably, 44 of his 53 wickets – 84 per cent – were caught by a fieldsman or the 'keeper, reflecting a lack of penetration with the ball.

Skull also played World Series Cricket, and in the second year of Packer cricket he toured the West Indies.

Each morning pace bowler Mick Malone and Skull would leave the team hotel early for a run. They would come to a set of lights or a busy corner and Mick would consistently yell, 'Look out, Skull!'

It got to the stage when Skull ignored Mick's warnings. Then one day the bloke who was calling wolf really did have a concern for his teammate.

'Look out, Skull!' he yelled.

Too late. O'Keeffe was run over and he wound up in hospital with a broken leg.

Kerry O'Keeffe was a good all-round cricketer and finding his niche at the microphone was perfect for his career after cricket.

MALCOLM FRANCKE

The Jack Russell of spin

Malcolm Francke was one of the best spinners of the period. A leg spinner, he toiled brilliantly for Queensland after migrating to Australia from Sri Lanka via England, where he had worked for a few years after leaving his homeland. An accountant, Francke worked in England and played league cricket. He was offered a chance to play in the English County Championship, but the pay on offer was poor. So he opted to make his home in Australia, where he continued to work as an accountant, and played cricket with Queensland with the hope of getting a Test cap.

Malcolm was born on 21 March 1939, a stone's throw from the famous Mount Lavinia Hotel, a grand colonial structure built in 1805. The hotel is a favourite haunt for tourists, a delightful palatial building that, along with the Galle Face Hotel along Colombo's waterfront, would have been something of a sundowner oasis in the colonial past, when Sri Lanka was Ceylon.

Francke played some good cricket in Australia. He wasn't a big spinner of the ball, but he got it to bounce, and, while he didn't turn his leg break to a great degree, he had a good top spinner and a splendid wrong'un. As a bowler he was like a Jack Russell – when he sensed a kill he went for it. Champion Test batsman Greg Chappell, who was Francke's Queensland captain for a number of seasons, held him in high regard.

'Malcolm was a very good bowler and much underrated, especially by Doug Walters and Ian Chappell, who always tried to belt the shit out of him,' he recalls.

> They rarely succeeded in doing so and regularly got out to him. He bowled a bit quicker than most (leg spinners) and bowled with lots of over spin, so he got good bounce which often brought the better players undone. I always felt that I was in the game at slip.

Chappell added that Francke bowled well in Brisbane and in Perth because of his over spin. Because of his lack of side spin his leggie didn't spin much, which he turned into a strength by attacking the stumps. 'Malcolm bowled very few bad balls and had more belief in his ability to get out good players than most leggies,' Chappell says.

> I think he was unlucky not to have played some Test cricket because he seemed to lift against the better players. Not something that could be said for most leg spinners (of the period). Malcolm was a particularly good fieldsman from his own bowling, which was a surprise because he wasn't a brilliant fielder otherwise.
>
> Malcolm always thought he didn't get the opportunity to play Test cricket because he was coloured, but I don't agree. I think it was because he was underrated and a bit misunderstood. I think that his age told against him. Considering that he was many years older than he claimed to be, his fitness levels and record was commendable.

As a leading spinner in Australia at the time I believed Francke to be desperately unlucky not to have played a few Test matches. I don't think he would have let his adopted country down.

Francke played representative cricket for Ceylon, as Sri Lanka was still known, in 1956–57, but the games he played were deemed first-class, as the country had not at the time been given Test-match status. He started for Queensland in 1971–72, making his debut against the touring World XI team led by Garry Sobers. The World XI was put together in a hurry in the wake of the South African tour being suspended due to the republic's continuing racist policy preventing any non-white cricketer playing for the national team. In that match at the Gabba Francke bowled superbly, dismissing Clive Lloyd (twice), plus Rohan Kanhai and the great Indian opener Sunil Gavaskar.

He took 167 first-class wickets for Queensland with an innings-best of 6/62 against South Australia in 1974. While Francke continued to enjoy consistent success for Queensland, he was continually ignored by the Test selectors. In 1977 Ian Chappell wrote that Francke 'was a very steady type of spinner, with good line and length, but I can't really see him bowling out Test batsmen. As well he is getting on in years.'

In 1975 Francke was part of a rebel tour of South Africa, playing for the Brian Close–led DH Robins Eleven.

Surprisingly Francke returned to the Queensland side in 1985–86, some six years after everyone thought the leg spinner had played his last first-class match.

In September 2018 Malcolm Francke was one of 49 former Sri Lanka cricketers honoured by Sri Lankan Cricket for their services before the nation became a full member of the International Cricket Council. In all of his 61 first-class matches Francke took a total of 178 wickets at 31.02 with the 6/62 against SA in 1974 the best of his eight five-wicket hauls. He also took 31 catches and is remembered for his enthusiasm, all-out aggression and persistence. Malcolm Francke was the epitome of energy. He scurried about, sometimes giving lip to opposition players, especially if they happened to be leg spinners: the mortal enemy. To me, Francke was the Jack Russell of spin: ever on the hunt.

TONY MANN

The boy wonder spinner

For more years than the locusts have eaten, fast bowlers have abounded in Western Australia. On the flint-hard pitches in the west few spinners got much of a bowl in state cricket. There was scope for spinners in grade cricket, but none in the 1950s were really putting up their hand to command a regular state berth. Then along came Anthony Longford Mann, a young leg spinner with the Midland Guildford club. From 1959, when he was 14, Mann was the spin sensation of Western Australian cricket. Like a young Shane Warne, Tony spun his stock leg break fiercely, such purchase did he achieve that the ball fairly hummed on its dipping trajectory towards the batsman.

As juniors Tony and I played against one another, Tony for Midland Guildford against me at Mt Lawley. He always bowled from the end at which his father, Jack Mann, the umpire, stood. Jack Mann, founder of Houghton Winery, was a pioneer in the WA wine industry, creating in 1937 the Houghton White Burgundy, now the White Classic, one of Australia's most popular drops. Jack built a global reputation at Houghton Winery for excellence. He was chief winemaker at Houghton from 1937 to 1974 and was awarded the MBE in 1964.

Umpiring junior cricket was a breeze for Jack. When Tony got a ball to spin and take the edge, or to hit the pads, Jack smiled broadly as if to say 'That's my boy!' and he would gleefully raise the index finger of his left hand. On weekdays after school Tony, older brother Dorham, younger brother Bill and neighbour Dennis Yagmich played backyard Test matches on the Mann family verandah. Tony bowled, Dorham or Bill batted and Dennis crouched behind the wicket, supposedly there to snare a catch or a stumping but the boys were all too aware that Yagmich's main role was to prevent any ball getting past him and careering into Angela Mann's patch of prize geraniums.

Dennis Yagmich rarely conceded a bye in those verandah matches. No wonder he went on to keep wicket for WA, then SA. Before Tony turned 13 he used the orthodox off-break as his variety ball to his stock leggie. At that time, in 1958, he taught himself to bowl the wrong'un and it happened as he experimented on the brick verandah of the family home.

That 1958–59 season Tony continued playing senior cricket with Middle Swan and he took 93 wickets, eclipsing the record set by his father years before. Jack had been left with a disabled right arm after a shooting accident and he was forced to bowl underarm: leg breaks.

Soon after Tony's record-breaking summer for Middle Swan seniors, two Midland Guildford stalwarts and WA sporting heroes, Keith 'Spud' Slater and Kevin Gartrell, called in to see Jack Mann. They were on a mission to coax him into allowing his son to play A grade senior cricket for Midland Guildford.

'Dad thought I was too young for such a step,' Tony recalled, 'but Spud and Garty were persuasive and Dad finally agreed.'

In his first A grade match for Midland Guildford against a strong Subiaco batting line-up Tony, who played in white shorts and sandshoes, bowled 14 eight-ball overs and took 6/29. My Nedlands baseball mentor, Neville Pratt, a WA and Australian baseballer and Subiaco's opening bowler, told me: 'That boy Tony Mann will play for Australia. I'm sure of it.'

Next grade game for Midland Guildford, Tony took two cheap wickets against Claremont Cottesloe, the only wickets to fall before the tea break. He stood with the other players at the tea pavilion, but Tony was wearing his shorts and the lady pouring the tea from a large container said softly, 'Now dear, you'll have to wait until the players have finished their afternoon tea.'

Tony has not forgotten the moment: 'Spud took me by the arm and came back to the afternoon tea area and said to the lady, "Now this fellow Tony Mann is our best bowler. He's earned a well-deserved refreshment." Mrs Wakefield and I became very good friends afterwards,' Tony laughed.

At university Tony played alongside John Inverarity and Rod Marsh. Both men saw the genius in young Mann's bowling. It was at university that Tony was given the tag 'Rocket'. Brilliant at cover, Mann had a rocket arm. The term stuck: the nickname was made for him.

Former Midland, WA and Test opener Wally Edwards remembers:

Tony's father, Jack, was my first coach and gave me a good start from about the age of 12. I remember Jack saying, 'Tony loves to go kangaroo hunting. He is a very good shot and usually only requires one bullet to get the job done. So to give the roos a bit of a chance he doesn't take a gun anymore. He just takes a bag of cricket balls and knocks them over with his bullet throw.'

Rod Marsh kept to Mann at university and for WA.

'Rocket Mann was a heck of a good leggie in his early days,' Marsh recalls.

> I would say the fact that he had such a good wrong'un was the start of his demise. He used his wrong'un too much as he knew few could pick it and as a result he lost his excellent leggie.
>
> The fact that he got so many wickets with his wrong'un was bad for his bowling in my opinion. His playing for Bacup in the leagues in England didn't help. He would have bowled with a wet ball and just tried to contain. The last I remember him bowling in Sheffield Shield cricket he still had the wrong'un but his leggie wasn't really threatening. What a shame! Batsmen eventually realised the difference between his leggie and his wrong'un as the different ball was his leg break!

Near the end of his career the great Neil Harvey batted for an invitation side against the WA Governor's XI at the WACA in the early 1960s. Tony deceived Harvey with a beautifully flighted wrong'un, which dipped sharply and the ball spun away from the great left-hander, leaving Harvey stranded well down the wicket as Marsh joyfully whipped off the bails.

That was some coup for the youngster, for in his 79 Tests, many of which were against the wiles of fabulous slow bowlers such as Jim Laker, Tony Lock, Sonny Ramadhin, Lance Gibbs and Hugh Tayfield, and despite making a habit of charging down the track to spinners, Harvey had never been stumped in any of his 137 innings.

Marsh, Inverarity and WA all-rounder Ian Brayshaw are at one about the Mann wrong'un. They believe, as do I, that Rocket's heavy dependence on the wrong'un was detrimental to his wicket-taking capabilities. His strength had become his weakness. Yet Rocket himself has no regrets about the way he went about his bowling. Maybe Stuart MacGill got things right. MacGill had a superb wrong'un in his armoury, but he used it rarely and it became a brilliantly effective shock weapon.

Rocket Mann was nevertheless a very good first-class cricketer for WA, playing 80 matches, scoring 2544 runs at 24.22 and taking 200 wickets at 34.54 runs apiece. The best of five five-wicket hauls was his 6/94 for WA against SA on the Adelaide Oval. And wouldn't you know: in that innings he trapped me plumb lbw with his wrong'un!

Neville Pratt's prediction came true: Rocket did play for Australia, four Tests in all, against India Down Under in 1977–78, a series played in fierce opposition to Kerry Packer's World Series Cricket. He took just 4/316 at an average of 79, but it was his 105 in Perth that was the highlight of his brief Test career. Rocket had gone in at the fall of the first wicket, becoming the second nightwatchman in Test history, after Pakistan's Nasim-ul-Ghani, to score a century, and his effort enabled Australia to successfully chase the 339 needed for victory.

Rocket never got to bowl the 'Midland Hanger', the special ball of Bunny Gartrell, Kevin Gartrell's father, a ball that WG Grace so successful lobbed all those years ago. The 'Midland Hanger' was a high-flung delivery, designed to land squarely on the top of the bails.

'I probably did bowl the odd Midland Hanger … but never on purpose!' Tony says.

Rocket was lucky to have come under the influence of Slater and Gartrell and later Norm O'Neill and Barry Richards, all of whom gave such great service to Midland Guildford CC. Throughout his cricket career Rocket Mann batted, bowled and fielded with such obvious joy and never-ending enthusiasm. He was the boy wonder of spin bowling, who enjoyed bowling his wrong'un a bit too much.

TERRY JENNER

Shane Warne's mentor

Terry Jenner hailed from Corrigin, a little country town 200 kilometres south of Perth. There Arthur Jenner, his father, ran the general store. TJ grew up full of confidence. In country cricket he was a wicketkeeper but he yearned to become a leg spin bowler. His father and mother split up and his mother, Queenie, came to live in a house in Mt Lawley, an older established suburb not far from the Perth CBD and just a stone's throw from the Mt Lawley Cricket Club's home ground, Shearn Park. In the summer of 1959 our latest recruit to the club was a skinny, gangling country boy wearing a big baggy brown peaked cricket hat, which was clearly too big for him. The 14-year-old newcomer was leaning on the side wall of our ancient wooden pavilion. There was something about this young bloke. He was confident and when I extended my hand in welcome he told me straight away, 'I'm a wicketkeeper now … but I aim to be a good leg spinner: the best.'

Ah, I thought, every 'keeper thinks they can bowl leg breaks. Terry spoke as though the world was his oyster. He exuded confidence, probably the legacy of his old man, Arthur.

One day at his 'local' Arthur hit triple 20 with his first two darts and instead of 'following his dart' as would all top pub players, Arthur invited all the drinkers at the bar to the corner where 'you can watch me make it 180!' Arthur had a propensity to boast and would turn his back before the dart hit the board. He knew where it was heading. Terry was pretty cocky, like his old man.

At the time TJ arrived at the club I was the star emerging spinner, so when TJ began to show terrific skills with his leg breaks there began a very competitive rivalry between us that continued throughout our cricket careers.

In the early 1960s I was playing fourth grade for Mt Lawley and TJ was above me in the thirds. We got lots of bowling then and we improved, although it was not until we were coached by Tony Lock and received invitations to junior state squads and matches run by John Rutherford that our cricket improved markedly. John Rutherford became Western Australia's first Test player in 1956, the year he toured England, playing one Test in Bombay on the journey home. In the early 1960s he ran a WA Colts squad and lives in a town on the wheatbelt in WA – until a year or so ago he turned out once a summer, batting for a local team wearing his 1956 baggy green. John is now in his 90th year.

There was a time when Tony Lock coached a group of 12 spinners in a special squad at the WACA ground. Among that group were four youngsters who went on to play Test cricket: Terry Jenner, left-arm spinner John Inverarity, Tony Mann and me. Inverarity was a handy spin bowler, but mainly a specialist batsman. TJ played A grade cricket before the rest of us. Once he hit 60 not out batting at No 11. I joined him in the A grade side a year later, opening the batting and getting an occasional stint at the bowling crease. TJ batted in the middle order and bowled only after the likes of speedsters Trevor Bidstrup and Tony Mateljan, fast-medium bowler Graeme John, left-arm medium pacer Jack Richards and the main spinner Ron Frankish.

Before TJ and I happened along the spin was mostly handled by Frankish and sometimes Graham 'Snake' Farrell. Frankish was a quickish off spinner who had developed the doosra – a leg break with an off-break release – before the word was coined. But Ron, as with all the rest in later years, had to bend and straighten his arm to deliver it. In those days we called it a 'chuck'.

Despite a lack of long spells at the crease in grade cricket TJ's bowling came on fast.

During a training session at the WACA ground nets ex-WA leg spinner Tony Zimbulis, who had played 14 games for the state in the 1930s, taught TJ how to bowl a wrong'un. TJ loved this delivery and he used it wisely, not bowling too many. In grade cricket he began to excel and deservedly won a place in the WA team quickly.

He made the WA side at the age of 18, but with Tony Lock, and sometimes Tony Mann, in the side, there wasn't much hope of hours and hours at the crease. To maintain his spot in the side TJ had to get runs in the lower order and field well.

There was an outward confidence about TJ and an abundance of bluff to his cricket. One Saturday, TJ and I were batting together for Mt Lawley against Subiaco, who had in their midst the raw pace of left-hander Jim Hubble. He was bowling quick and short to TJ. Each ball got progressively shorter and one bounced higher, forcing TJ so far back that he trod on his stumps, one bail falling to the ground. Thinking quickly like a modern-day WG Grace, TJ quickly looked at the square leg umpire, Warren Carter, who, not unusually, happened to be looking anywhere but the actual play, so TJ nonchalantly leaned over, replaced the bail and settled over his bat for the next ball.

'Jeez, TJ, you can't do that!' I blurted. But he could, and did.

There was plenty of bluff about my spinning mate. He had charisma and seemingly could talk his way out of any difficult situation.

The next season TJ found himself the team's captain. I had no idea of what was going on behind the scenes, but TJ was quite the lobbyist. He knew how to get his way.

In our first match TJ was still dragging on a cigarette as we took the field. Umpire Warren Carter had TJ hauled before the tribunal and he was fined one guinea.

As Umpire Carter later explained: 'One drag was enough and Terry told me he would put it out. But then he had a last drag and that was too much.'

TJ and I lived for cricket. On Sundays we played for a club called Miling, some 200 kilometres north of Perth. The competition had five teams and we got Miling into the final four for the first time in 50 years. We played on malthoid pitches and when it got hot – and let me tell you, the town of Miling in summer was red hot – the rubber in the malthoid bubbled, and the ball spun and bounced so much our 'keeper stood five yards back from the stumps.

When either of us lured a batsman down the track and he missed the ball, our 'keeper would take the ball cleanly, but he never could stump anyone with a shy at the stumps. The batsman always retrieved his ground safely. So soon enough when TJ bowled I kept wicket and when I bowled he kept. Often the grounds we played on were rock hard and sometimes a fire was lit to clean the stubble from the outfield.

TJ, as we shall see, became quite the cricket coach, but his first attempt at coaching was a disaster. There was TJ giving Miling Cricket Club's three brothers – Ray, Des and Les White – instruction on how best to defend their wicket against a big, burly fast bowler.

Each of the White brothers was clean bowled first ball. Surely this was the only time identical triplets – all clean bowled – had featured in a hat-trick. Yet playing under TJ's captaincy I realised that he possessed a fabulous cricket brain and he knew how to get the best out of his team.

As a bowler he knew what he must do, how to plan a batsman's demise, but he became frustrated at times because he could not execute the plan.

TJ first came up against Les Favell, the South Australian opening batsman and skipper, during a match in Perth. WA captain Barry Shepherd threw TJ the ball and before he had started to move in to bowl Favell was singing 'Happy birthday to me!'

Favell charged down the track like Victor Trumper and hit the ball over cover for four. Shepherd sent John Parker to field on the fence.

Favell was still singing 'Happy birthday to me' when TJ moved in for his second ball. Again the ball went over cover, first bounce to Parker on the boundary.

Non-striker Ian Chappell raced through for the run, but when he arrived, Favell, with his back turned to him, and his bat behind the popping crease, yelled: 'Piss off Chappelli, it's my birthday, not yours!'

TJ learned two things about becoming a spinner. You needed patience and you had to have a sense of humour.

It was during WA's eastern tour of NSW, Queensland and SA that TJ began to think about a move interstate. During the Shield match at Adelaide he received an offer from the strong Prospect Cricket Club in Adelaide. I had been 12th man for WA and TJ had played 30-odd state matches, but with Lock in the WA team we had to go elsewhere. We picked South Australia. Favell was an attacking captain and SA had no spinners.

First we decided to make a few dollars to fund our train trip to Adelaide. We landed a job for a week as cleaners at a large office block in Leederville, close to the city.

What a calamity. TJ made me chief security officer, the keeper of the keys and head latrine cleaner. He gave himself the important role of cleaning the upstairs hallway and drafting office with a huge, hard-to-handle, industrial polisher. Our cleaning had to begin when the last of the office workers had left the building. One of those characters happened to be accountant Peter Kelly, one of the incumbent WA opening batsmen and TJ's state teammate.

First night I heard this almighty crash. I rushed upstairs and there was TJ leaning forlornly over the industrial cleaner. It had careered out of his grasp and through the big plate glass window of the drafting office.

I consoled him.

'Insurance claim, mate, no problem.'

Next morning, the woman who hired us was okay with our situation and confirmed that the insurance would indeed cover the damage.

Next night's work went perfectly. Then just as the lift doors opened TJ threw the bunch of keys to the keeper of the keys and I dropped them. They fell straight down the liftwell gap. This time we had to ring our employer at 10 pm to arrange for someone to bring a spare set of keys.

We sensed our employer's patience was beginning to wear a little thin.

On the third night we mopped and polished the linoleum floor of the drafting office. Then TJ found a makeshift bat and ball that the workers used for a bit of entertainment during their lunch break.

We began to have a hit and a bowl when a late worker came into the room. He slipped on the polished floor and landed heavily on his back. We figured we had used too much wax. 'Bit of a sticky wicket, eh, mate?' TJ laughed.

Thankfully the bloke saw the funny side and our employer never got to hear about that one.

On the last night we decided to start late. We took a couple of girls to the trots at Perth's Gloucester Park. We began work at around 10 pm and neighbours complained about the lights of the office block still being on at 1 am.

When we got to the job agency to collect our pay the woman said, 'I know you had girls at the office block on your last night.'

She reached into a drawer and pulled out a purse and said, 'Make sure that young lady gets this back. I am not going to dock you any money, but I just hope your cricket turns out better than your cleaning detail.'

After a stint at Ayr in Scotland, I too joined the Prospect club. I found digs at the home of Lorna Gilbourne, whose son Bob played for the club, and later the state. He was in one bed, me the other. Then TJ came to stay. He was given a mattress on the floor. Soon after, when Bob got married, TJ got the vacant bed.

We found the Adelaide Oval pitch turned and bounced for most of the match and we figured that the side needed two spinners, certainly for home matches.

And we were fortunate beyond all measure to get lessons from the great Clarrie Grimmett. The old craftsman emphasised getting the ball above the batsman's eyes, and he proved decisive in the development of us both as spin bowlers.

Playing for Prospect against Glenelg in a one-day match was a pointer to things to come. TJ dismissed Greg Chappell and I got his brother Ian, so the state selectors may have become a little interested. I missed the first Shield match of the season with a dislocated finger, but TJ played and he grabbed a five-wicket haul.

He loved captain Les Favell's attitude.

'After I went for a few too many runs in my first couple of overs, I thought I'd be taken off,' TJ told me. 'But it wasn't at all like my experience with WA. Les would place his hand on my shoulder and say in a fatherly tone, "C'mon son, give me one good over and you're on for the session."'

TJ Jenner (right) with me, his spin twin, Ashley Mallett. (ASHLEY MALLETT
COLLECTION)

Soon TJ and I were playing together for the SA team and bowling in tandem. We became the 'spin twins'.

For years we bowled in tandem, at Mt Lawley in Perth, for Prospect, in South Australia and, on occasion, for Australia in Tests.

We rarely talked strategy, but in the field I used to watch him like a hawk. He could work a player out. You sort of got the feeling that a wicket was going to fall. I recall TJ bowling to a left-hander at Adelaide Oval one day. I was fielding at backward square. TJ was spinning the ball up and the leftie was using his feet, getting down the wicket, driving quite forcefully on the off side – one or two to mid-off, one or two to cover.

'Time for a wrong'un, old boy,' I thought.

It came that very next ball. The bloke was stumped, yards out of his crease.

After the game we enjoyed soaking up the atmosphere in the company of such luminaries as Ian Chappell, Les Favell, Barry Jarman and Neil Hawke. Favell and Jarman treated us like family.

If TJ reckoned Ian Chappell gave me too much of a go and he had been ignored, he would front the skipper at the end of play. TJ heralded his arrival one day by thumping the long-neck bottle of beer on the table where Chappelli was sitting. The captain said, 'Okay TJ, what's the problem?'

TJ wanted to know why he hadn't been given a single over.

Chappelli asked him whether he wanted an answer that would soothe his temper or whether he wanted the truth.

'The truth,' TJ answered.

'To tell you the truth, I forgot you were out there,' Chappelli answered.

While he craved a better relationship with his dad, TJ always received great support from his mother, Queenie, and his sister, Lorraine.

189

The day I paid $90 for my first car, a gleaming 1956 FJ Holden, I drove TJ and Queenie to Scarborough Beach in Perth. We all sat together on the front bench seat, but the seat gave way. TJ and Queenie ended up tumbling backwards and TJ maintains that it was a miracle I hung on to the steering wheel.

Another memorable day, in 1960, TJ and I were walking from training at the WACA nets. There was a match just completed involving the Governor's XI. It was the last dramatic day of the first Test against the West Indies in Brisbane. As we walked towards the pavilion a shining black Rolls-Royce limousine came to a stop beside us. The back door opened and a voice called out.

'Hop in boys. It is the last over and Australia looks like winning.'

And there we sat, listening to the ABC broadcast of Wes Hall bowling that famous final over of the Tied Test match in Governor Sir Charles Gardiner's Rolls.

After his cricket career was over, TJ tried a number of things, including selling cars. He also got trapped in the addictive world of gambling and fell into a spiral of debt and even more gambling to repay the mounting debts. It all ended in his being convicted of embezzlement and being sent to prison. Ian Chappell visited TJ in jail and came to the conclusion that if TJ could turn his life around he'd 'make a damned good coach'.

Rod Marsh, director of the Australian Cricket Academy, agreed to give TJ a go at the academy as one of his spin bowling coaches.

There he linked up with the young Shane Warne. They were alike in personality. You just knew Warne was special; he had that sparkle in his eye, much the same as TJ had as a youngster.

'Shane's like a sponge,' TJ used to say. 'The most coachable spinner of them all.'

TJ's genius as a coach was in being able to get his message across loud and clear. People know how good he was at illustrating a point or telling a good yarn. He did that beautifully when commentating on ABC radio, giving a speech or running his famous TJ Test Match brekkies. Spin bowling was his passion and he lived and breathed the art. He taught Warne a lot.

When Warne talks spin on television his passion shines. He talks of how in his first few overs he used to bowl to stay on, keeping things tight and not having to play catch-up if he went for a few runs early. This was TJ's philosophy. Warne talks of 'spinning up', another phrase that was commonly on TJ's tongue.

Terrence James Jenner was a terrific cricketer who was always spinning a ball or a yarn, usually to do with the game of cricket. He played nine Test matches, the first against England in Brisbane in late 1970, the last against the Windies, also in Brisbane, in late 1975, taking 24 wickets at 31, his best return being 5/90 against the West Indies in the Caribbean. In Sheffield Shield Cricket for WA and SA he took well over 250 wickets.

In Warne he found a brilliant talent who certainly could and did execute his plans to dismiss batsmen the world over. As a coach TJ found the perfect path to help others by sharing his broad knowledge of the art of slow bowling.

Cricket and the magic of spin were his passion in life. He passed away in Adelaide in 2011 aged 66 after a long illness.

ASHLEY MALLETT

'Give up bowling and become a batsman!'

I left school at the age of 15. That was the done thing in the early sixties. The parents who came through the harrowing days of the Great Depression, of which mine were among the many thousands, had a specific view of job security. My father, Ray, spent all of his time during the Depression working for the Bank of New South Wales. He loved figures and wanted to push his sons in that direction.

'Get a job in a bank or the post office,' he'd say. 'You don't have to work at all and they give you a cheque at the end of the week.'

Good advice, Dad.

My form master at Mt Lawley High School in Perth, Don Melrose, asked me what I intended to do when I left in 1960.

'Well, Don, I am going to play Test cricket and I intend on becoming a good writer.'

His usually thick lips narrowed to a pencil line and he said with a tinge of relish, 'Ah, ha, that's not on. There is no money in cricket and you are hopeless at English.'

He was right on the first score. There certainly was no money in cricket before Kerry Packer happened along. And I wasn't too brilliant in the area of grammar. But I got by and improved with a bit of common sense. If the words sounded right, in context, and with a certain rhythm, sentences would turn out just fine.

My working journey began in the Commonwealth Bank in Perth. It was a particularly boring job, the only solace being the daily discussions round the table over lunch and contributing to the bank's suggestion box.

At lunch the conversational topics were always the same.

In summer it was cricket, sex and how to rob the bank. In winter it changed slightly to football, sex and how to rob the bank. Stories about how staffers would attempt to steal from the bank went from partly true to rather embellished to totally false, but luncheon was always a bright and breezy place to shoot the breeze. The story was told of one bloke in the main branch in the Perth CBD whose job was to count out money boxes, in the days when people would drop in their filled money boxes. You may recall the Commonwealth Bank money boxes, which were green and required a can-opener to get to the coins.

This fellow always had a large rubber mat stationed under his stool. He would take the box and tell the customer, 'Leave me with the money box and your bank book and I will have the money counted and deposited in your account.'

Banks were trusted establishments in those days.

What the money box man allegedly used to do was to spread all the coins on his desk top and drop some in a large box and others would land on the rubber mat. 'One for you … one for me.'

The bank was not for me, but it did provide some good material for future writing.

Cricket was my main aim. And I gained the greatest inspiration when my grandfather Alec 'Pop' West took me to the Sydney

Cricket Ground to watch the last day's play of the second Ashes Test in the summer of 1954–55. I was then aged nine.

Pop and I sat right on the pickets in front of the MA Noble Stand at the Paddington end. Australia needed only 230 or thereabouts to win the match and I guess Pop thought it a good introduction for his grandson to see an Aussie victory. As it turned out Frank 'Typhoon' Tyson bowled like the wind and cut the Australian batting to ribbons with a six-wicket demolition job.

Only Neil Harvey (92 not out) took on the English attack, but he simply ran out of partners. During that hectic day's play a young, plump Englishman named Colin Cowdrey was fielding on the third-man boundary almost within arm's reach of me and Pop. Fourteen years later Cowdrey became my first Test wicket at The Oval in 1968.

Not long after that Sydney Test there was huge upheaval in the Mallett household.

Dad announced that we were moving to Perth. It was a big wrench for Mum, for she would be leaving behind her father, two sisters and brother. We sailed to Perth in a P&O liner, the *Stratheden*, and upon arrival in Perth we stayed in the Palace Hotel, one of the best hotels in Perth, which in those days was like a big country town. To me it was akin to landing on the moon: many, many miles from anywhere, a lifetime away from family and friends. You couldn't even buy a Streets Paddle Pop. But children are resilient.

In 1956 the England off spinner Jim Laker took an incredible 19/90 against Ian Johnson's Australian team and I was hooked. My pathway to the Test team would be as an off spinner. I joined the Mt Lawley Cricket Club in Perth. Initially I had tried to bowl like Tyson – fast – but I soon realised my body was not and never would be built for speed. So I stuck to off spin.

But I also taught myself to spin a leg break and as I progressed through the ranks to the club's fourth-grade side I'd bowl off-breaks one day and if they didn't turn out too well I would bowl my leggies.

My first Test wicket; trapping England captain Colin Cowdrey lbw with my fifth ball on the first day of the Ashes fifth Test at The Oval, August 1968. (ASHLEY MALLETT COLLECTION)

In winter I played for the Nedlands Baseball Club. The youngsters were indeed lucky, for our coach was none other than Charlie Puckett, a legend of the game and a pretty good cricketer. It all changed for me when the baseball league changed baseball from a winter sport to a summer one. My father recognised that I had to make a choice. 'It's baseball or cricket, son.'

I didn't know which one to pick for I was much better at baseball than cricket.

'Which game do you like playing best?' Dad asked.

'Cricket,' I said without hesitation.

'Okay, cricket it is … wasn't difficult was it?'

I graduated up the grades for Mt Lawley, had a couple of carnivals with the state schoolboys' team and finally got a game in the A grade at the age of 16.

But I had one problem – my bowling.

I was in various state and special squads, including one 12-strong squad under the tutelage of Tony Lock. However, while I was tight, rarely giving too many runs away, I wasn't rapt at consistently failing to grab a bag of wickets. Then I happened upon a book Pop had posted to me from Sydney. It has been mentioned before in these pages: *A Century of Cricketers* by AG 'Johnnie' Moyes.

The story on one player, Clarrie Grimmett, really hit home. Here was a man who played 248 first-class matches and took five wickets or more 127 times. 'Wow,' I thought, 'I could learn a lot from this man.'

Heartily sick of constant failure I knew I was not a good bowler out of luck, as I had kept telling myself for a couple of seasons, so I decided to write to Mr Grimmett and seek his help.

Despite my lack of success I was picked as 12th man a couple of times for WA in 1966–67, the summer before I boarded the train to see Mr Grimmett at his Adelaide home.

I turned up at his splendid house in leafy Firle, about 8 kilometres east of Adelaide and knocked on the front door.

Mr Grimmett's wife, Lizzy, opened the door and said abruptly, 'Get off the porch, I've just washed it.'

Order was soon restored and she told me Mr Grimmett was waiting for me.

'You'll hear some sawing of branches. I think he's up a tree.'

As I turned the corner of the house the 76-year-old legend sprang from the tree and before introductions could be completed he handed me a Jack Hobbs Autograph cricket bat.

Grimmett had a cricket ball in a stocking suspended from a branch of that peppercorn tree.

'Now let's have a look at your batting.'

He could sense my hesitation.

'Don't worry, son. I taught a young man to back cut on board the ship bound for England in 1930 ... and Don Bradman was a fast learner!'

I played one ball.

'That's enough of your batting,' he said. 'Let me see you bowl.'

The old spin legend led me to his backyard cricket pitch. It was a full-size turf wicket.

Mr Grimmett wore street clothes, no gloves, no protector, no pads, just his cricket bat.

'Bowl up, son.'

I carefully measured out my run-up and bowled the first ball.

It met the full face of his cricket bat. He beckoned me to meet him halfway down the pitch.

'Son, give up bowling and become a batsman ... I could play you blindfolded.'

'I have a handkerchief here Mr Grimmett,' I volunteered, determined that the spin legend wasn't going to shrug me off that easily. He put the kerchief over his horn-rimmed glasses.

The second ball again met the middle of his bat and when he stopped laughing he proceeded to give a brilliant lesson in flight, talking with passion about how a hard-spun ball coming at the batsman just above eye level was the key to this spinning business.

I recognised then that to get good players out on good pitches one had to beat them in the air.

'It is not really about where the ball lands, but how it arrives, ideally hard spun and dipping,' was his overall message.

Just before catching the train from Perth to seek help from Grimmett, I had found work as the professional-cum-groundsman at the Ayr Cricket Club in Scotland.

Armed with my new-found spin-bowling wisdom, I took wickets aplenty. Sure the standard wasn't brilliant, but there were plenty of ex-county and Test players from different parts of the world playing in the Western Union and I was getting stacks of wickets.

During my stint there, I negotiated a weekly sports column with the *Ayr Advertiser*, the editor promising me £5. I thought that my summer's 22 1500-word articles educating the Scots about the game of Australian Rules football would net me the grand total of £110. Maybe I should have stayed in the bank after all, because at season's end the editor presented me with a crisp £5 note for my summer's writing.

My cricket was on song and I thought the writing experience would somehow work for me down the track. After flying back to Perth, I found that I was still in the WA state squad, but I knew I had no hope of playing for WA while Tony Lock was the incumbent spinner, with little cameo appearances from Terry Jenner and Tony Mann well ahead of me, or so I perceived the pecking order. One day at training I asked state selector Wally Edwards what chance I might have of playing for WA in the coming season.

'Well, Ash,' he said, 'We see you as vying with Ian Brayshaw for the all-rounder's spot.'

'There is only one problem with that, Wally.'

'Oh …?'

'I can't bat, so I'm going to Adelaide where I reckon I'll get a game straight away.'

After a season with SA I was picked in the 1968 Australian team to tour England and was involved in a series with the West Indies in 1968–69 – the same year SA won the Sheffield Shield and then toured Ceylon (yet to be renamed Sri Lanka), India and South Africa. In India I played in all five Tests and took 28 wickets at 19 runs apiece. After the tour I sought to find a decent career, as one had to complement cricket in those days.

I accepted a job as an advertising salesman. A salesman I was not, but I got to sell the odd ad after convincing the shop owners that editorial with the ad was a godsend. It worked and I loved the writing part. An opportunity in the editorial team soon eventuated.

I opted out of the 1972–73 Australian Test tour of the West Indies purely because I wanted to get into journalism. I did and it was a terrific experience. I covered all manner of subjects: council, parliament, police rounds. I wrote colour and hard-news pieces and did all-round general reporting. The day I retired from cricket in 1981, Geoff Jones, chief of staff at *The News* in Adelaide, offered me a job as a general reporter.

In the Test team I had four tours of England, and one each of Sri Lanka, India, South Africa and New Zealand.

Marrying work with cricket was always an increasingly frustrating juggling act. Some of the Test players worked at a big bank or a cigarette company where they were well looked after; others were school teachers so they could save up holidays.

I missed a lot of cricket during my career and the only time I received a decent payday was one summer with World Series cricket.

After 15 years as a journalist I reckoned I had enough confidence and ability to do as I had always yearned to do: write books. I left *The News* and went freelance, but to increase my annual wage I got

Me bowling at Lord's Cricket Ground, 1972. (ASHLEY MALLETT COLLECTION)

into coaching. That took me round the world, to England, South Africa, India, Sri Lanka and New Zealand. This is my 33rd book. Not all have been cricket books, but many have been.

Running Spin Australia, I have had the great pleasure of working with the likes of Tim May, Shane Warne (albeit briefly), Stuart MacGill, Steve O'Keefe, Greg Matthews, Murray Bennett, Ashton Agar and Nathan Lyon. Then there's players from other nations: New Zealand's Daniel Vettori and Jeetan Patel, South Africa's Pat Symcox and Paul Adams, Sri Lanka's Rangana Herath and England's Gareth Batty, Monty Panesar and Graeme Swann.

There is always pleasure in the acknowledgement that I have helped out a fellow spinner. An email from Graeme Swann when he retired from Test cricket was particularly pleasing.

> Having a man with your knowledge and keen eye look out for me over the years has been invaluable for me. I have worked with many coaches over the years but you stand above them all in your expertise of off spin bowling and I feel lucky to have met you and learned from you. I loved every minute of my Test career. Coming in at a time when finger spin was seen as such a defensive, negative tool I was always sceptical about how far I could go attacking as much as possible, especially in a four-man attack. I'm glad I stuck to my guns and had guys like you watching out for me when things slipped in my technique.

Perhaps when I get back to London, or when Swanny returns to Australia, we can have a chat about the magic of spin over a cold one or two.

JIM HIGGS

A Gladstone bag and a cut lunch

Jim Higgs was the best leg spinner Australia produced after Benaud and before Warne. A laconic character, Jim was pretty much a throwback to old-time leg spinners who gave the ball a big tweak and tossed 'em high, inviting the batsman to drive. He had a bit of a gangling shuffle to the crease and a long, sweeping bowling arm. Jim was no elite athlete; his batting was below par and his fielding was the very antithesis of his splendid bowling, which included hard-spun leg breaks, fizzing top-spinners and a pretty good wrong'un and flipper.

Jim was born at Kyabram, in country Victoria, on 11 July 1950. He played club cricket for University and Richmond and made his first-class debut for Victoria in 1970–71.

He earned his nickname early in his career. Jim would arrive with his gear in a Gladstone bag – and so his nickname became 'Glad'. In my mind's eye I can still see Jim arriving at the ground with a Gladstone bag and a cut lunch. He had one other peculiarity: if someone happened to ask him a question with an obvious answer, he would say, 'Can a duck swim?'

When Victoria won its 24th Sheffield Shield in 1979–80 it was Higgs's magnificent bowling that won the day. All the planets aligned with his deliveries and he got the ball to do everything but talk. The magic of spin brought South Australia undone. At lunch of the final day, the South Australians were cruising towards victory with Ian Chappell in brilliant form. Straight after lunch Higgs came on at the scoreboard end of the Adelaide Oval and began a magic spell of top-class leg spin. He got the ball to fizz, turn and bounce enough to beat Chappell, but not his glove and not the 'keeper Ritchie Robinson. Jim took 6/57 off 20 overs of some of the best collection of leg breaks, top-spinners, wrong'uns and flippers you'd ever wish to see.

Jim toured England in 1975, but did not play a Test match. However, he did have a few good days against the county sides. That was with the ball, not so much the bat. He didn't even fit the well-known saying, 'Jim scored one in the first innings and wasn't so successful in the second.' On the 1975 tour Higgs faced just one ball, from off spinner Ray Illingworth. He played forward and met the ball in the middle of his bat. Jim was an engineer by profession and knew all the angles, but on this occasion his bat was so acutely angled that the ball ran down the face of his bat onto the turf, spinning back to hit his stumps. Captain Ian Chappell and a few of the older hands thought it might be something if Higgs didn't score a run on tour. And he did not. Whenever Jim looked like facing a ball the skipper declared.

Higgs got a second chance at Test cricket when Kerry Packer's World Series Cricket divided Australian cricket. He made his Test debut under Bob Simpson against the West Indies in Port of Spain in 1978, toured India, then played against England at home.

Things got tougher for Jim when the WSC players returned. He played two of the six Tests against the Windies and England in the 1979–80 summer.

That magical spell in the Shield final caused captains, coaches and selectors to see his ability in a fresher, perhaps kinder, light. He bowled well enough on tours of the West Indies and India and against New Zealand and India when they toured in 1980–81 and probably should have beaten Kerry O'Keeffe and Ray Bright for a spot on the 1981 Australian tour of England as the No 1 spinner. But that was not to be.

Some pundits reckoned Higgs's Test chances were limited because the selectors of the day preferred the safer option of tighter finger spinners. However, more to the point, Higgs's fielding was under par and his batting was hopeless. He simply had to be one helluva bowler to command a regular Test spot without any sort of back-up abilities. Being able to hold up an end with the bat was important, and fielding was probably more vital to a team's success. You often got the impression that Higgs was not exactly switched on in the field. He was so laid back that you could be forgiven for thinking that Glad had actually fallen asleep.

In 22 Tests he took 66 wickets at 31.16. He scored just 111 runs at an average of 5.55. That is higher than his first-class average of 5.4, earned over 122 matches that produced 384 runs. His highest Test score was 16 – although he played one knock more memorable.

Batting was never his forte, but he worked hard on it, not developing an array of shots to produce a flurry of runs, but a solid forward and backward defence to deny the opposition his wicket long enough to allow the man at the other end to make some runs. So it came to pass during the Boxing Day Test against New Zealand at the MCG in 1980 Higgs sauntered to the wicket to join Doug Walters. The score was 9/261 and Walters had just passed 50. For some extraordinary reason the Australian Cricket Board had decreed that an umpire could call no-ball if he thought a bowler was bowling with 'intimidatory intent'. The score gradually mounted and Higgs hung in there ... blocking everything. Walters's total mounted, 70, 75 … 80 … A century beckoned and the Kiwi players were getting frustrated. Medium-pacer Lance Cairns bowled Higgs a bouncer and Jim tried to fend it off, but succeeded only in snicking a catch to the keeper. Umpire Robin Bailhache yelled 'No-ball.'

This cute – or stupid – rule meant Higgs survived. In fact, he stayed long enough for Walters to complete his hundred. It was Higgs (6 not out, 61 balls in 96 minutes) who ran out of partners the moment Walters was clean bowled by Jeremy Coney for 107. The pair had put on 60 runs. When the game ended in a draw New Zealand was 6/122 – 65 runs short of victory.

After he retired as a player Glad became a Test selector. He also did some coaching and was among the first coaches to advise the emerging star Shane Warne.

Jim Higgs was unique: highly intelligent and a clever spin bowler, the best leg spinner in the interregnum between Benaud and Warne.

RAY BRIGHT

Tough, stoic, loyal

Ray Bright was born on 13 July, the same day as Julius Caesar, albeit a few years down the track. He was never given credence as a leader in the Caesar mould, but he did – for a time – serve as vice-captain to Allan Border. A tough little cricketer, Bright was a left-arm orthodox spinner. Courageous and a hard to shift down-the-list batsman, he was a fine fieldsman and a splendid team man. He played 25 Tests, taking just 53 wickets at 41.13 and scoring 445 runs at 14.35 with a highest score of 33. He scored two centuries in first-class cricket.

Bright made many a tour with Australia and his crowning glory as a bowler was his 7/87 against Imran Khan's Pakistan in 1980. Gideon Haigh once wrote of him: 'For a time Ray Bright was colloquially and rather meanly known for having made almost as many tours as he had played Tests.' He performed brilliantly for Ian Chappell's Australian team during the stormy days of World Series Cricket, playing 15 Supertests for a return of 42 wickets at an average of 29 against the mighty batting line-ups of the West Indies and the World XI.

On the eve of the last day's play in the Australia–India first Test at Chennai in 1986, Bright decided not to join some of the others for a nightcap of cold beers, but went to his room and ordered a pizza. Bad mistake. He was crook as a dog all night and was still pale and shivering with a fever on that definitive final day. He later said: 'Who orders a pizza in India?'

He bowled in tandem with Greg Matthews for most of that last day. The temperature rose beyond 40 degrees in the old money; there was a blanket of 90 per cent humidity and right next to the ground was a dirty canal, the constant stench of which wafted over the ground.

Matthews said Bright's stoic performance of taking 5/94 that last day to help him (5/146) bowl India out for 347 and record Test cricket's second tie in history was the 'most courageous performance I have seen on a cricket field'. That was the same Test in which Dean Jones lost 8 kilograms sweating while making a double century.

For Victoria Bright always bowled well against Greg Chappell, but struggled to contain Ian Chappell and other free-scoring batsmen who used their feet deftly. Bright, nicknamed 'Candles', shone by his determination and stoicism. He was a good deputy to Border and when AB threatened to step down from the captaincy during a bleak period for Australian cricket in the 1980s, Bright called the rest of the team together to ensure AB continued as their leader.

Julius Caesar could have done with a like show of loyalty from his senators.

BRUCE YARDLEY

The epitome of energy

Bruce Yardley had been a bits-and-pieces cricketer before he found his niche by ditching his medium pacers and concentrating on his brilliant slower ball, which was a hard-spun, dipping off-break.

I played baseball against Bruce, who was nicknamed 'Roo'. He had a thin and wiry build akin to a shearer's kangaroo dog, which was pruned to what became a term of endearment, 'Roo', which happily overlapped with 'Brooce'. He played for Swan Districts as a pitcher and I played for the Nedlands Baseball Club as a pitcher.

The year is 1960 and we are the opposing pitchers in a final; the winner's prize is a spot in the grand final. Nedlands had bases loaded, and two down in the ninth inning; an ideal moment for their pitcher to step up to the plate. Roo used to throw a good outcurve, which was effectively a chucked off-break. I swung and had a bit of luck hitting a home run to win the match. Years later I reminded Roo of the day, but he couldn't recall any details. That says it all: Bruce Yardley dealt only with the positives of life. He was the most enthusiastic cricketer of my experience.

One day at the WACA ground in Perth Roo bowled me a terrific off-break as a change-up slower ball to his lively medium pacers. He had long strong fingers and got the ball to bounce more than most finger spinners. His Midland Guildford A grade teammate Keith 'Spud' Slater, a brilliant footballer, WA and Test cricketer, suggested Roo change and become an off spinner. Spud must have seen what I saw. Roo's slower ball, an offie, was his best delivery. Why not bowl it all the time?

It must have been around the mid 1970s when Roo first bowled offies in a Sheffield Shield match. He bowled one to me and it dipped wickedly, spun and bounced. I managed to get a huge snick on a beautifully flighted ball and the dolly of a catch was swallowed by Bruce Laird at forward short leg.

Ah, a fellow offie was Roo's first first-class wicket with an off-break. But no. As I walked from the crease, I happened to look back and see Umpire Crapp with his head down, shaking it vigorously. Evidently I didn't hit the ball. Much to the chagrin of Rod Marsh and Dennis Lillee, I turned on my heel and scurried back to the batting crease.

WA deservedly won the match. Roo got a few wickets and he was on his way.

Apart from his off spinners, which were usually more effective on the faster wickets in Brisbane and Perth, Roo was a brilliant fieldsman and a daring, hard-hitting, if unorthodox, lower-order batsman. It was during the World Series Cricket revolution that tore the game asunder in the Australian summer of 1977–78 that Roo got his chance to play Test cricket for Australia. While the cream of Australian cricketers were battling the West Indies and the World XI in a pace-dominated series, the Australian Test team, skippered by Bobby Simpson, took on India in what became a saga of spin. Roo replaced fellow West Australian Tony Mann for the Adelaide fifth Test. He failed to capture a wicket in the Indian first innings, but took an impressive 4/134 in the visitors' second innings to help Australia to a historic series victory.

In 33 Tests Yardley took 126 wickets at 31.6 and scored 978 runs at 19.76.

As a batsman he often stepped away from the fast bowlers and slashed the ball over slips or gully. It proved an effective ploy and he scored many a useful run in hurricane fashion.

His half-century against the West Indies at Kensington Oval in Bridgetown 1978 was the fastest Test 50 by an Australian player – and the record stood until David Warner came along.

Roo got to 50 off 29 balls. To make it even better, Roo copped nasty blows to the elbow, throat and toe while throwing his bat at everything. At the other end Joel Garner crushed the batting efforts of Steve Rixon, Jeff Thomson and Wayne Clarke and Yardley was left with perennial 'rabbit' Jim Higgs. But the Victorian leg spinner somehow hung on for 27 minutes, facing 24 balls, time enough for Yardley to bring up his 50 with a hook for six. He ended up undefeated on 74. In that match Graham Yallop became the first batsman to wear a full protective helmet in Test cricket. Roo wasn't wearing one.

He made a surprising comeback to the WA side in 1989 in his 42nd year. However, his comeback didn't last long. I recall him telling me: 'Rowd, they train at the nets and then run you into the ground, with endless sprints, push-ups, sprints which all added up to … exhaustion.'

'Once a sports psychologist addressed us. He said if you put a plank across the gap between two buildings at 40 storeys you might be intimidated to walk the plank. Yes, I am sure of it,' he laughed. 'But if you put the same plank between two bricks six inches high it would be easy to cross with confidence. Wow, the guy was a genius. Then the fellow came up to me and sat down next to me in the dressing-room.

'Roo, I just want to …'

Yardley cut the man short, stood up and walked off, with the retort, 'Don't mess with my head man. I just want to bat, bowl and field.'

Roo was of the old school. He didn't want any of what he called 'the psychological mumbo-jumbo that sportsmen and -women have to endure' in the modern era, when really a good dollop of common sense would do the job.

After his playing days Roo did a few stints of commentary on the game, working on the Nine Network in Tasmania's first hosting of a Test match. But his main thing was coaching in Sri Lanka and recognising the sensational ability of Muttiah Muralitharan, the freakish off spinner who went on to take the most wickets – 800 – in Test match history.

Roo never lost faith in Murali. He was his mentor and encouraged the Sri Lanka whiz to bowl his doosra. While others castigated Murali, Roo kept the faith.

Roo was an amazing cricketer – vibrant, energetic, a terrific team man.

He bowled his way. He spun the ball with the middle finger rather than the index finger, the favoured spin finger utilised by most offies.

Yardley was on top of his game mentally; the epitome of energy and a brilliant unpredictable all-rounder.

GREG MATTHEWS

A different breed of cat

It was during Bobby Simpson's reign as Test coach that I first set eyes on Greg Matthews. I had been asked by Simmo to have a look at Matthews bowl in the Adelaide nets. 'Don't be fooled by his funny haircut, earring and John Lennon–style sunglasses. He's very different, but he is a good cricketer,' Simmo said with a smile.

Apparently the nickname 'Mo' somehow sprang from Greg's call of misére in the game of 500. As I recall we had someone batting in a net as Mo bounced up to me, thrust out his right hand and said, 'Hey, Thrash. How's it going man. And how am I bowling?'

'Well, I am going okay, but just how well you are bowling, I haven't a clue. I've not seen you bowl a ball yet.'

I worked with Mo for a number of years. Technically he was a good off spinner and got heaps of wickets for NSW, especially on his beloved Sydney Cricket Ground wicket, which throughout the 1980s was, as they say in the trade, a 'Bunsen' (Bunsen burner, meaning in Cockney slang, 'turner'). Yes, the SCG wicket spun like a top. Many spinners who played for NSW in the period tended to undercut the ball. They got the ball to turn consistently, but when they played on the harder surfaces of Adelaide and Perth they struggled to make a big impact. Mo often bowled with his cap on, something that would have warmed the heart of Clarrie Grimmett, who always bowled with a cap on. But then Clarrie was bald as a badger from a young age.

Mo was a stickler about being set at the top of his mark before he approached the wicket. He had a good sideways action and he completed it with a sweep of his bowling arm past his left knee. Classic. Mark Taylor was Mo's favourite captain, for the NSW (and later Test) captain let Mo run. Mo was unafraid to plough his own furrow and, while he was ever eccentric, funky, slightly rebellious, bordering on the punk, he respected the game of cricket and its traditions. He usually wore a long-sleeve shirt, the sleeves wider than usual, flapping in the breeze as he moved.

'Some guys chew gum. Some chew their nails. Some abuse their teammates. I played air guitar. I sang to the crowd. I sang to myself and I danced. I said things to the good sorts in the crowd. Can someone please tell me what's wrong with that?' Matthews once told *Inside Sport*.

That attitude provoked conflicting views about the man. One of his Test captains, Greg Chappell, said Matthews was the strangest cricketer he ever play alongside.

'He came from a different background, spoke a different language, a surfie's language', Chappell said, '"bro", "cool" being a major part of his language. He didn't meet the stereotype of what an Australian cricketer looked like, spoke like, sounded like. And yet he had a love of the game that was as strong as anyone I ever played with or against.'

In the amazing first Test match of the 1985–86 summer at the Gabba between New Zealand and Australia, when Richard Hadlee took 15 Australian wickets (9/52 and 6/71), Matthews struck a brilliant 115 in 205 balls in Australia's second dig. He endeared himself to the nation when he slog swept to reach his century. Immediately he dropped his bat and rushed past the startled bowler, the non-striker and the umpire towards the square leg boundary where his girlfriend, Jillian Clarke, was sitting. 'She stood up and waved me to go back because I was going to jump the fence and put one on her. I then drew an imaginary M for my mum to let her know I was thinking of her.'

Mo wheeled away for NSW and established a terrific Sheffield Shield record. Maybe if he had played more Tests under someone such as Mark Taylor he might have done better on the Test stage. But his greatest day in the sun in international cricket came in September 1986 at Chennai. Australia batted first and amassed 7/574 declared. Dean Jones hit a remarkable 210, David Boon 122 and Allan Border 104. Matthews scored 44.

Mo bowled 28.2 overs in the Indian first dig, taking 5/103 including the prized wickets of Sunil Gavaskar, Ravi Shashtri and Kapil Dev.

Batting a second time Australia went for quick runs and declared at 5/170, Matthews 27 not out. The Indians had to score 348 in their second innings to win the match. There were two balls remaining in Matthews' 40th over. India was 9/347, one run from victory. Australia could only lose it or tie it. This was Mo's big chance to become a hero to his nation – or the guy who lost the Test. He was bowling to the Indian No 11 Maninder Singh, who had lasted three balls in the over. Ravi Shastri (48 not out) could only watch from the other end.

Mo moved in with purpose. Umpire V Vikramraju crouched low. The pressure was on him too.

I have watched many replays of that last vital ball. It dipped in flight on a line just outside the right-hander's off stump. Maninder was stuck on the crease. No sooner had Matthews' off-break crashed into the Indian's pads than Umpire Vikramraju shot his right index finger skywards at great speed. Out.

Cricket history is made: it is a tie. The second tie played in 1052 Test matches.

Matthews said Vikramraju was 'the most courageous umpire on the face of the earth'. He was standing in only his second Test. It was also his last. Even captain Allan Border later admitted there may have been the hint of an inside edge on the ball.

Dean Jones famously made 210 in that match, which was to that point the highest score by an Australian in a Test in India. His knock lasted 503 minutes in searing, energy-sapping heat. After his innings ended Jones was rushed to hospital and put on a saline drip. Exhaustion and dehydration had conspired to lay him low. He says that even decades later his body begins to shake when the temperature gets above 37 degrees – the memory of the agony has never left him. And while so many people laud Jones's efforts, Mo has a different take: 'He got runs on an absolute road. Please, get over it.' Matthews much preferred the effort of a fever-ridden Ray Bright taking five wickets in tandem with himself on the last day.

Mo's 5/146 followed his first innings 5/103 – the one and only time he took a 10-wicket haul in a Test match.

The Australian captain Allan Border praised Matthews for his stamina and skill, especially on the tension-packed final day. 'Under those conditions for Greg to have bowled more than 30 overs and end up with a 10-wicket match haul was just a magnificent performance.'

Teammate Steve Waugh was similarly impressed, writing that his 'stamina and resilience were absolutely staggering'. It is notable on the footage that Matthews wore a sleeveless sweater while in the field and *two* while bowling. Waugh lets us in on the secret – Matthews' theory was that nomadic herders wore woolen clothes, as they kept cool air in, so he did the same.

In 33 Tests Matthews scored 1849 runs at 41.08, with four hundreds and 12 fifties: statistically a batting performance in the same league as Mark Waugh (Test average 41.81). With the ball, Mo's figures were in the end disappointing, taking 61 wickets at 48.22. But taken overall as an all-rounder, Matthews was one of Australia's best. His weakness was his slower ball: it was too easy to pick, and the likes of England's Mike Gatting charged down the track at the hint of a Mo slower one, usually getting it on the full and dispatching it to the boundary.

Nearing the end of Bill O'Reilly's long and illustrious career as a cricket correspondent, we spoke during an Ashes Test at the MCG. Matthews was in the Australian team and O'Reilly was staying at the same hotel as the players. At breakfast one morning, O'Reilly met Matthews. They spoke for a matter of minutes then went their separate ways from the breakfast buffet.

'Now, son,' Bill said to me in a serious tone. 'Is Greg Matthews the full potato?'

Matthews has delighted listeners on radio and viewers on television with his zany commentary. And he has done some good work coaching emerging cricketers. In addition he has been a close supporter and worker for the Australian Cricketers' Association.

In the mid 1980s he was reputed to have knocked back two attempts to lure him into Kim Hughes's rebel Australian side that toured South Africa. The purse was a cool $200,000 a season, supposedly tax-free thanks to some loophole.

Mo's response was 'no thanks', saying $200,000 'wouldn't make me happy'. I suspect he simply wanted to don the baggy green cap he loved so much.

The zany off spinner called fellow spinners brothers. If they were off the long run, cutting the ball rather than spinning it, Mo would be totally dismissive. Once I was co-opted to have a look at the action of Queenslander Geoff Foley, who was called for throwing after turning away from medium pace and taking up off spin. I found his gangling, awkward action okay when he had a short delivery stride, but when he stretched out, he appeared to throw the ball. No matter to Mo. He said to me, 'Thrash, this guy Foley is not one of us; he's not in the brotherhood!'

Yes, Mo was a different breed of cat. He was also a tough, dedicated cricketer with commitment, flair, loyalty and consistency. Greg Matthews did not bow to convention. He did things his way.

THE SHANE
WARNE ERA

By the mid 1980s spin bowling was in a bad place, lagging way behind the rampaging speedsters of the West Indies and likewise overlooked in every other country trying to follow suit. Globally the art of spin bowling was shoved aside for later contemplation, perhaps, or tossed in the too-hard basket. Then Shane Keith Warne burst onto the first-class scene like a spinning gift from the cricketing gods. His example put an end to ludicrous misconceptions about spin and spinners. For example: if, let's say, David Boon square cut a lively Richard Hadlee short ball to the fence, it was a magnificent shot. But, on the other hand, if Boon skipped down the track to, say, England off spinner John Emburey and hit him one bounce over mid-on to the fence, it was a 'bad ball'. Just before Warne bestrode the Test stage there were spinners of the ilk of Greg Matthews and Tim May, who both had their time as the flavour of the month. Then came Warne and everything changed. The cricket world as we knew it was different. The pacemen were not suddenly shoved aside, but teams started to look about for this new breed of bowler: the spinner. The too-hard baskets were emptied and examined. Some bowlers who were discarded or forgotten or both suddenly reappeared. Suddenly captains and coaches of this modern era started to believe that spin bowling had a place in the Test match stage.

TIM MAY

His version of magic

One summer's day in the late 1970s the astute cricket coach Chester Bennett was putting a group of young cricketers through their paces at the Adelaide Oval indoor centre. On that day I spotted a young off spinner named Tim May, from Prince Alfred College, one of Adelaide's most prestigious private schools. This youngster spun the ball hard and even at the age of 15, as he was then, he had good control of the ball. He was on the road towards dipping hard-spun deliveries with a tantalising flight. Rarely does one look at someone so young and predict big things for them, but I found myself saying, 'Chester, this young bloke Tim May ... he'll play for Australia one day. I am sure of it.'

May had a faltering, stumbling type of approach to the wicket, but once he got to the bowling crease he assumed a side-on position, so much so that his back was almost presented to the batsman. His delivery stride was very short, but very soon into his first-class career he had command of his line and length. He spun the ball so hard he often had trouble with his spinning right index finger, but he had lots of stamina and bowled long spells, not just shoring up an end, but getting wickets at a consistent rate. A captain could rely on May to bowl consistently well to his field, thus taking care of one end, allowing the skipper to rotate his faster bowlers in short, fiery bursts at the other.

During a tour of Australia in the 1980s, just before May made his state debut, I spoke to off spinner John Emburey, who was sitting out the state match against South Australia at the Adelaide Oval. I asked 'Embers' if he wouldn't mind having a chat to a young man who I believed was destined to become a champion off spinner. And I asked Emburey if he would wouldn't mind me listening in to the talk. 'Not at all, Rowdy,' Emburey agreed.

We sat at ground level just back from the fence on those great old wooden-slatted benches. The sun shone and the play created a great atmosphere for Embers to come forth with some wise words. 'Now, young Tim,' he said, 'I don't try and get anyone out for the first four overs.' I couldn't let that one go.

'Okay if I say something,' I interrupted.

Emburey nodded.

'Mate, I must tell you that in one Test match in Brisbane against the West Indies, the then captain Bill Lawry gave me four overs in three spells.'

We all laughed. Emburey was trying to emphasise the importance of not trying too much too early, thus establishing pressure on the batsmen and not having to play catch-up.

I always felt it was a good idea to bowl to stay on and that meant to keep things tight, bowl hard-spun stock balls at varying paces and build the pressure. Soon Tim was playing for South Australia and early on he was impressing good judges with his skill. He made his Test debut in December 1987 against New Zealand at the Adelaide Oval. The Kiwis batted brilliantly in their first innings with Andrew Jones (150) and Martin Crowe (137) figuring in a blazing partnership to ensure a 400-plus first innings. May bowled a marathon 54 overs for a return of 1/134. It appeared to me that Tim was bowling too straight a line. After the NZ innings I asked Crowe why he didn't try to hit May through the covers. 'No way,' he said. 'The lad dips and spins the ball so much I just waited for him to get too straight and he did that too often, so I could work him on the on side for easy runs. When he gets his line right, he will be something ...'

May toured England with the Australian side in 1989, but he didn't make an impression. He played just 10 first-class matches on tour, bowling 287.5 overs and taking 28 wickets at 26.42. His main rival for a Test spot was the Queensland leg spinner Trevor Hohns. May struggled for a time to get wickets consistently. Mind you, he maintained his sense of humour, probably a must for any spinner. There was a bomb scare at the team hotel in London and during the evacuation May was asked about the trauma of the event. 'Well, bombs are great levellers, you know,' he said deadpan.

Back in Australia after the England tour, he, and others, believed there was something wrong with his action, but in reality he was operating from the same spot on the bowling crease and at the same pace. He put an enormous amount of spin on the ball, got it to dip awkwardly in flight, and bounce. That hadn't changed. All that was required was to bowl a little smarter: use the crease and change his pace. By the time his next tour of England came in 1993, May was the complete off spinner; the best I've seen since WWII.

Tim May came into the side for the second Test at Lord's and his partnership with Warne – who had bowled *that* ball to Mike Gatting in the previous Test – was a revelation. Australia hit an impressive 4/632 declared. Then Australia set about dismantling the England batting. May bowled brilliantly. Operating from the Members' end, he clean bowled Gatting with a ball that curved away and spun through the gate to bowl him for five. Poor Gatting, he must have thought the cricketing gods were conspiring against him.

May had Robin Smith stumped by Ian Healy for 22, with a ball that skipped away from the right-hander, to finish with 2/64 off 31 overs.

He deserved better figures, but we all know figures don't always tell the full story. Warne took 4/57 off 35 overs and the two Australian spinners bowling in tandem were a joy to watch. In the second innings May took 4/81 off 51 overs and Warne 4/102 off 48.5 overs, the Australians winning by an innings and 62 runs. May bowled 278 overs in the four Tests he played in the series, taking 21 wickets at 28.19, and Warne bowled 439.5 overs for a return of 34 wickets at 25.79.

May and Warne proved to be the best Australian spin bowling combination since the halcyon days of O'Reilly and Grimmett. It is a pity May didn't play in the new era, for he would have played many more Tests and captured hundreds of Test wickets. To my mind he was the best off spinner the nation has produced since Hugh Trumble.

In the end he played 24 Tests, taking 75 wickets at 34.74. In today's cricket, batsmen the world over have forgotten the art of footwork against good-quality spin bowling. There is a stand-and-deliver attitude, so the spinners can employ an 'in-out' field – a few in close for the edge, the rest prowling near the boundary. The combination of T20 cricket, big bats and smaller grounds has conspired to bring this about. Had May played in today's Test cricket he would undoubtedly grabbed wickets like they were going out of fashion. Even in May's time, long after the World Series Cricket revolution, a cricketer's salary was often not enough – work beckoned, for May had to maintain a liveable salary, and so it was that his Test career ended after eight years, at the New Year's SCG Test against England in 1995.

May retained an active role after retiring by becoming the inaugural CEO of the Australian Cricketers' Association in 1997, and latterly the chief executive of the Federation of International Players' Associations. He resigned from the Australian job in 2005 to move to the United States with his wife, but stayed in the international post.

Tim May dismissed the best players of his time enough times to prove he was as good as or better than any off spinner to turn out for Australia in a Test match. He gave the nation his own tantalising version of the magic of spin.

●

STUART MACGILL

He did it his way

If Shane Warne was the master leg spinner of the modern era, Stuart MacGill was the apprentice. As Warne spun his way into cricket immortality, MacGill spun his leg breaks, toppies and big wrong'uns with such an attacking mindset he too captured the imagination of the cricketing public. In 44 Tests from 1998 to 2008, MacGill took 208 wickets at 29.02 with 12 bags of five wickets and two hauls of 10 wickets in a match. He was a huge spinner of the leg break, but that was not always the case.

When Stuart was about 18 he was among a group of emerging spinners in Perth and, as part of my international coaching program, Spin Australia, I was working with them at the WACA ground nets. As it happened, it was not the first time I'd encountered a cricketing MacGill; in the late 1960s I played a Sheffield Shield match or two against Stuart's father, Terry, who played 12 first-class matches for WA. In the nets that day Stuart got the ball to buzz alright, but he bowled mostly fizzing top-spinners and a terrific wrong'un, which spun and bounced. His leg break was almost non-existent.

The MacGill bowling arm was too high to enable him to get his wrist in the right position. I asked him why he was bowling with such a high arm.

'I aim to get the ball to angle in and spin away,' he said.

'Well, mate, you are getting the ball to angle in, but you are not spinning away. There are two things you can do, Stuart. You can ask the batsman to stand at backward point, that way your wrist will be in perfect position to deliver a good leg break or ...'

'Yeah I know ... bowl with a lower bowling arm.'

Once he cottoned on that the amount of spin a bowler imparts on his leg break makes the ball curve in towards the right-hand batsman, Stuart MacGill was away.

Stuart was born in Mt Lawley, WA, on 25 February 1971 and his full name is Stuart Charles Glyndwr MacGill – SCG MacGill. He left WA early in his career to play for NSW and what a fitting set of initials. He loved the SCG and many of his greatest spinning days were performed on that famous arena. I got to see him at the Australian Cricket Academy run by Rod Marsh and noted how much he was getting on his leg break: the bowling arm was lower, much lower than it was when I first set eyes on him in Perth.

Stuart made his international debut in the third Test against South Africa in the summer of 1997–98. The South Africans scored more than 500 on the true Adelaide pitch and MacGill and Warne got lots of bowling. MacGill finished with 2/112 off 29 overs. His first wicket was a good'un; Jacques Kallis lbw for 15 and Warne took 2/95 from 33 overs. In the second dig MacGill grabbed 3/22 off seven overs and Warne 1/52 off 15 overs. The match was drawn thanks to an unbeaten 169 by Mark Taylor in the Australian first innings. But the game was significant in that MacGill had shown enormous potential at the highest level.

During Warne's drugs ban in 2003–04 MacGill had his chance to shine. And shine he did, taking 53 wickets in 11 Tests.

Stuart MacGill delivers a ball to Bangladeshi batsman Mohammad Rafique (unseen) during the second day of the first Test match between Bangladesh and Australia at the Osmani Stadium in Narayanganj on 10 April 2006. MacGill took six wickets as Bangladesh scored 427 runs all out in the first innings. (FARJANA K. GODHULY/AFP/GETTY IMAGES)

Some criticised him for conceding at least one boundary ball an over. Before Warne happened along, a boundary or two off a wrist spinner seemed the accepted norm, so why all the fuss? MacGill was no Shane Warne and he never tried to emulate him. He simply did what he did to the best of his ability, and that was pretty damned good.

MacGill was another cricketer who wasn't bound by convention. He did it his way; his way or not at all. He wasn't the greatest of batsmen, nor was he a terrific athletic fieldsman. Unlike Warne, who was the full package as a cricketer – wonderful bowler, good down-the-list batsman, excellent slips fielder – MacGill hung his hat on his bowling alone. His career ended when he was diagnosed with carpal tunnel syndrome of his bowling wrist after the Australian side returned home after a tour of Sri Lanka. He underwent surgery, but his bowling lost its bite and he hung up his boots.

A wine connoisseur, MacGill hosted a pay television show called *Uncorked* and he learned later in life to enjoy the taste of beer. In this he resembled Clarrie Grimmett, who was only introduced to beer at the age of 44, by none other than Bill O'Reilly on a tour of South Africa. However, Clarrie's earlier drink of choice was tea, not wine.

On a tour of Pakistan MacGill once managed to read 24 novels. That suggests he had no time to mess about drinking with his teammates. He refused to tour Zimbabwe in 2004 because of the oppressive Mugabe regime, showing his consciousness of a wider world beyond cricket. Along with Steve Waugh and other luminaries of politics and sport, Stuart MacGill is a board member of the SCG Trust.

As with Warne, MacGill has always ploughed his own field; did things his way without fear or favour. He is always up for a chat over a chilled glass of chardonnay or a decent red and is personable, gregarious and bouncing with energy. Stuart MacGill did himself – and Australia – proud.

SHANE WARNE

The magician

Shane Warne emerged out of the wilderness and arrived on the Test stage in the nick of time. Spin bowling the world over was struggling. Few of the cricketing nations could claim to have a spinner of genuine Test match class. The cupboard was bare, denuded by an onslaught of pace, the ravages of one-day cricket and sheer neglect. Many feared that quality leg spin bowling had gone the way of the dinosaurs and become extinct. Through a combination of skill, determination and panache, Warne changed all that. Suddenly all manner of people who had watched cricket before he arrived, people who did not know an off-break from a toothpick, were exposed to a whole new world. Suddenly the cricket world embraced the magical skill of this leg spinner. They flocked to the grounds or gathered round the telly to watch Warne bowl. It was just like the days of Richie Benaud: youngsters attempted to copy his style – the walk-up start, the eyes focused, the wrist cocked and the enormous surge of power through the crease. Warne had the unerring accuracy of a medium pacer, the ferocity of an express bowler and everything that most other spinners don't have: the ability to control the game and to control the batsman, and then dismiss him. He had the leg break, the top-spinner, the wrong'un – and the flipper, unsighted it seemed for a generation and more, passed to him in an unbroken chain from its creator, Clarrie Grimmett. Warne also had the zooter and the slider, which most people had never heard of. He changed the language of the game. He had drama. He had guile. He had psychology. How lucky was the generation of cricket followers who had the opportunity to sit and watch Shane Warne bowl from the comfort of their lounge rooms. If anyone doubted that the magic of spin truly existed, Warne was here to prove it did. He could make batsmen disappear. He had it all

But it was not always so.

Shane Keith Warne made his debut in the New Year's Test at the SCG in 1992. India batted once. Warne took 1/150.

He played the next Test, in Adelaide. A mere 23 overs over two innings failed to produce a wicket.

For the next Test, in Perth, he was 12th man.

He had two Tests to his name, and an appearance as 12th man, but only one Test wicket to his name – Ravi Shastri, out for 206. Warne knew he had to improve. Quickly.

So Warney got in his car and drove. He drove from Melbourne to Adelaide to see Terry Jenner. Who was about to become his mentor.

Warney was overweight. He wasn't anywhere near the bowler he wanted to be. He came to learn, and he had come to the right man. TJ was brutally honest with Warne, telling him he had all the toys to become a great cricketer – but he didn't know what to do with them.

It was in TJ's nature to tell it as it is: no bullshit. Many a player didn't appreciate his candour as coach, but TJ's method was perfect for Warne, who does.

'Shane, you bowl nicely and rip your leg spinners, you bowl your wrong'uns and your straight ones and you've got an unbelievable flipper. You also catch well and bat too. You've got the toys, mate, but you don't know how to use them. In other words, you don't know how to get people out.'

TJ then set about talking strategy. How to work a batsman across the crease, how to set a player up for the flipper to strike paydirt.

'Rowd, this guy listens. He absorbs everything I tell him then he goes away and tries stuff. The things that work he hangs on to; some stuff he discards,' TJ told me.

I used to love to see Warney spinning the ball from hand to hand. Never have I seen anyone snap a leg break as he did and he achieved it effortlessly. I used to think, 'God he's got to get his act together. He could be anything.' He has all that he needs to become the greatest leggie of all time.

TJ taught Warney how to use the crease: one ball from close to the stumps, then from a bit further away. TJ taught him how to work the lines: one or two balls on middle and leg, then middle, then off, then outside off.

Watching Warney set a player up for his brilliant flipper gave TJ such joy. How often did we see South Africa's Daryl Cullinan cut or pull Warne for a boundary, only to then repeat the shot – and find out too late it was the flipper, and he was clean bowled or out lbw. Cullinan was by no means the only one.

TJ always spoke with passion about the art of spin bowling, never more so than when talking about Warne. And Warney today is much the same. He delights in speaking about how to bowl to certain players, how to build pressure, how to execute ... how to nail the batsman.

It's the 1992 Boxing Day Test, against the West Indies. Warney is playing his fifth Test, at the MCG, before a huge crowd in his home town. The stage is set – and he is ready to take a significant step towards spin bowling fame.

A modest 1/65 was his return in the first innings. The Windies are 1/32 at the start of the fifth day, chasing 359.

I recall the Channel Nine cameras honing in on Warne at the start of the day's play.

'Now there's a young man who won't get much bowling today,' Bill Lawry said confidently in the commentary box.

Bill was right, Warney didn't bowl a great deal; just 23 overs and two balls. Twenty-three overs that brought a fabulous Test wicket haul of 7/52 and won a Test.

He clean bowled captain Richie Richardson with a magnificent flipper. Richardson played back and the ball scooted through low to slam into the middle stump. While Warney knocked over many a top-line player with his flipper, the one he got Richardson with that day at the MCG in 1992 might well have been his best.

Warne now had a handle on the strategy of how to get batsmen out. He never looked back.

Shane Warne started with the basics: spin the ball hard and have it drop from above the batsman's eyes. Because of how it arrived at the batsman's end, his area of danger was huge. A spinner who does give the ball a big tweak has to be super-accurate, for his area of danger in comparison to Warne's is like a dinner plate compared to the dining table. Warne's arm-speed was as fast as Glenn McGrath's, so his energy went up and over his braced front leg rather than direct to an area, as does the fast bowler. Warne spent a lot of time on his front leg and that, allied to his wrist and great shoulder rotation, provided the big revolutions that excited thousands of fans for more than 15 years on the Test stage.

He had six deliveries: the leg break, top-spinner, wrong'un, flipper, slider and zooter. And each figured more than once in getting a famous wicket. His great attribute was his ability to break the rhythm of the batsman. He would bowl his stock ball for hours on end, each ball of slightly different pace. It was his subtle changes of pace, allied to his big spin and his patience, that consistently broke the rhythm of the batsman. Each delivery landed in a different spot. As you watched Warne weave his mastery over the batsman you figured that he was operating with pin-point accuracy. Maybe so, but just as importantly his great spin and changes of pace had him working to a huge area of danger. Players lost their way against him. His great spin got the ball to curve and they often found themselves with their bat a long way from their pads. He bamboozled them. He trapped them. He wore them down. He hunted them. Let's take a detailed look at each of those deliveries.

Leg Break

They called it the 'ball of the century' when Warne bowled that magnificent leg break to dismiss Mike Gatting at Old Trafford, Manchester, in 1993. It was his first Test match delivery on the tour.

No writer of fiction would have dared script that and expect to emerge with credibility intact. The chubby kid from Melbourne's first ball in a Test in England was perfection.

The ball hummed as it left Shane's hand. Gatting seemed to have it covered, but the great side-spin made the ball curve dramatically and late and Gatting found himself playing across his front pad. The ball pitched well outside the line of leg-stump. Upon pitching the ball spun past the flailing bat of Gatting like a striking cobra. It crashed into the top of the off stump. Gatting looked down the pitch in disbelief. Umpire Dickie Bird looked a bit nonplussed himself. The Australians mobbed Warne. As Gatting rolled his eyes skyward, he walked off Old Trafford shaking his head in disbelief.

Richie Benaud said simply, 'He's done it!'

The BBC commentators did not know what had happened.

The cricket world was stunned.

It was a freakish ball, which would have defeated anyone, a Don Bradman or a Victor Trumper, just as it beat Gatting. The Englishman did everything right; he had the ball covered in his forward defence, but the late curve towards the leg side confounded him. Only a batsman of no ability, like a Phil Tufnell, might have survived, for Tufnell would have been playing down the wrong line.

A leg break is spun over the wrist, the ball spinning from leg to off. When executed correctly the palm of the hand points directly at the batsman just after release. Warne had a couple of versions of his leg break. The one that got Gatting was a ball with lots of side spin, the seam angled towards the gully region. He also bowled a leg break with more top spin, the seam for this ball, his stock ball, angled towards first slip. The side-spinning leg break tends to bounce less than the top-spinning leggie, but will spin further. Warne usually bowled his leg break on the line of leg stump, so that if the batsman missed it, the ball would hit the stumps. Often he bowled to a line outside the leg stump to take advantage of rough spots. He was always attacking and searching for a batsman's weakness. Had Warne only had variations of the one ball – his leg break – and no other type of delivery, he would have been a champion of the Test stage.

That ball had a great impact on English cricket; the Old Country was reeling, bamboozled by this new leg-spin phenomenon.

The wrong'un

Shane Warne had just finished an enthralling battle with Sachin Tendulkar on the Adelaide Oval in December 1999. Tendulkar was given out caught by Justin Langer close in. The bat was clearly a long way from the ball. It was a poor umpiring decision. Warne rarely bowled a wrong'un to Tendulkar, for not only did he pick the change, Warne, unlike Stuart MacGill, didn't get a lot of work on his wrong'un, thus it didn't have too many revolutions on it, it did not drop dramatically and batsmen such as Tendulkar were down the track to hit the ball on the full or the half-volley. The dismissal brought the left-hander Sourav Ganguly to the crease. He was different. He would work Warne's leg breaks to the leg side, hitting with the spin from outside off stump. Ganguly got to 60 before Warne tossed up his wrong'un. The ball dipped a bit; Ganguly completely misread it. He came down the track to drive what he thought was a regulation leg break, but the ball dropped and turned away a fraction.

He missed it by a mile and Adam Gilchrist had the bails off in a flash. The wrong'un was not Warne's favourite ball. In fact he rarely bowled it. Unlike the leg break, which is bowled over the wrist, the wrong'un is bowled out of the back of the hand and when released properly the back of the hand faces the batsman.

When Warne bowled the wrong'un he found that it hurt his third finger and would take skin off if he bowled it too much. He had enormous power in his wrist and his right shoulder and found that he could impart extraordinary spin to a leg break or a top-spinner; not so the wrong'un, because his method required use of wrist, shoulder and fingers. Richie Benaud used to suffer from a sore and skinned spinning finger during his career and he did not get anywhere near the purchase on the ball Warne did, yet Warne's fingers today are as soft and as sound as though he had never spun a ball. He was the ultimate in wrist spin.

The top-spinner
Warne had a magnificent top-spinner. The ball is released with the seam pointing straight down the wicket. It is bowled completely over the wrist, no side spin at all, and it will loop and drop and carry on straight. The top-spinner usually achieves a lot of bounce. Warne gave all of his over-the-wrist deliveries a big rip and his

top-spinner dropped quickly and bounced high. It hurried through on the batsman.

It's the second innings of Australia's clash with South Africa, the second Test, January 1998. The South Africans have been completely outplayed, but they are trying to hold on for a draw. Warne has steadily spun his way through their line-up, but one stumbling block remains: the solid and seemingly impregnable Jacques Kallis. He repeatedly plays forward and anything on off stump he lets go, playing only deliveries pitched in line with his stumps. Balls outside the line of leg-stump he pads away. Warne to Kallis that day was almost a stalemate. Warne decides to go around the wicket, creating a huge angle across the batsman. Kallis plays solidly, taking care to let the wider deliveries go by and pad away anything outside the line of leg stump. Then Warne serves up a ripping top-spinner. The ball dips sharply. Kallis shapes to pad it away, then changes his mind: this ball is different, a bit flatter, a bit quicker, a bit straighter. Too late. The ball skims through the little gap between bat and pad and hits the middle stump. Kallis's defence had been immaculate, seemingly nothing was ever going to get through, but this one did ... Shane Warne's 300th Test wicket.

Warne's top-spinner was one of his favourite weapons. It fizzed and dropped and bounced. He rarely bowled the wrong'un. Instead of the wrong'un beating the bat of a left-hander by a long way, Warne preferred to use his top-spinner. That was more likely to catch the edge.

The flipper

Clarrie Grimmett invented the flipper between the wars, working on it for a decade before he bowled it in a match – and no-one bowled it better than Shane Warne. Grimmett passed on the flipper to SA leggie Bruce Dooland, who later taught Richie Benaud. Victorian batsman and part-time bowler Jack Potter showed Shane Warne how to bowl it when he was at the Australian Cricket Academy in Adelaide.

To bowl the flipper you hold the ball between your second finger and your thumb. If you can click your fingers you have an idea how to bowl the flipper, for it is just like clicking your fingers while holding a cricket ball. You can hold it with the seam parallel to the ground, or upright, so the ball can land either on the smooth part of the leather, or on the seam. To bowl the flipper effectively requires strength of fingers, and also greater arm speed than normal. Warne possessed such strength in his forearms, wrist and shoulders that he found this ball relatively easy to bowl and to control.

Long after I had retired from cricket I taught myself to bowl the flipper. A bit late, you might say – but it did come in handy for coaching. One day at the WACA ground Cullinan asked me to bowl him some flippers, so that next up against Warne he'd be in charge. At the time I was coaching a few of the South Africans, mainly off spinner Pat Symcox, and I explained to Daryl that my flippers were pretty gentle fare; nowhere near the sort of explosive stuff he could expect from Warne. He insisted, arguing that he needed to see how the ball left the hand. Later he said: 'Okay, now I pick Warne's flipper every time.' But picking the ball and actually playing the ball are two different things.

Likewise, bowling it is one thing; knowing when to bowl it is another. Warne did the same thing repeatedly to Cullinan and England's Alec Stewart, notably in Brisbane in 1994. Stewart hit Warne through the covers off the back foot. That boundary gave Stewart great confidence and he planned to hit the next shortish ball in a similar way. When the next short one came Stewart moved away to give himself room to hit through the off side – and the ball skidded on to smash into middle and off stumps. It was the flipper and he hadn't seen it coming. Warne set up Cullinan in a similar way a number of times: a boundary or two off the back foot, then the flipper and it was all over.

The zooter

The zooter is really a back-spinner, the palm of the hand shown to the batsman as the ball is spun backwards. When the ball lands it tends to skid on straight and stay low. This ball is particularly effective on a batsman who doesn't get well forward, and there is always the chance of an lbw when such a player is struck on the front pad with the zooter, especially on a slow, low track.

Such was the wicket when Australia played England at Old Trafford in June 1993. In the England second innings Alec Stewart had comfortably reached 11 with one boundary, when Warne bowled him the zooter. Stewart must have read the ball to be a flatter leg break, for he seemed to allow for turn. The ball was close to the off stump and Stewart expected to be able to cut the ball away with the turn. However, the zooter skipped off the pitch, straight and a little lower than he expected. He got a touch and Ian Healy completed the job.

While the ball is spun backwards, it is not held in the manner of a flipper. The zooter doesn't come off the wicket at anywhere near the pace of the flipper.

Depending upon the surface of the wicket, the zooter can sometimes skip off quickly or tend to hold up and lose pace. Either way it is a handy variation and another ball to help the bowler break the rhythm of the batsman.

The slider

Unlike the zooter, which is a slow back-spinner, the slider is pushed out of the front of the hand. It revolves slowly and tends to skid straight when it pitches. Sometimes it will fade slightly like a little in-swinger. This ball is very effective against the stodgy type of player who plays continually forward, but doesn't stretch far enough forward. Even a delivery hitting the front pad is a potential lbw wicket ball. In an ICC Trophy match at Colombo in 2002, Sanath Jayasuriya had hit 42 in 52 minutes with six boundaries when Warne bowled him the slider. Jayasuriya thought the ball would come on a lot quicker, with bounce, and turn in towards his stumps, but the left-hander was fooled by the pace, the lack of bounce and the fact that it didn't turn at all. He got a faint touch and the ball crashed into his stumps. Late in his fabulous career Warne bowled more and more sliders and fewer flippers. England's Ian Bell was a veritable sitting duck for Warne's slider. Bell typically played forward in nonchalant style. He didn't get far forward and didn't have very good judgement of length. When in doubt against a bowler like Warne, Bell leaned forward. He also failed to adjust swiftly enough to changes of pace. Warne found it easy to fool a batsman like Bell with changes of pace. The slider is just another little change, something to deceive the batsman between the big-turning leg breaks and the fizzing top-spinner.

At the age of 52 Ian Chappell, a brilliant player of spin bowling and a handy leg spinner himself in his day, jumped at the chance to bat against Warney, while coaching at the Australian Cricket Academy.

> It was a fascinating experience, enhanced by the fact that earlier that year (circa 1995) over a late-night beer at a house in Augusta, USA, I told him he would've had to bowl to me with a mid-wicket fieldsman on the boundary. Warne at Augusta as a guest of Channel Nine and sipping on a Midori was equally adamant he would not have needed a deep mid-wicket.

After a 20-minute net session at the Adelaide Oval indoor nets Chappelli conceded to Warney that he found him 'harder to hit to mid-wicket than I'd imagined'.

Shane Warne leaps in the air to bowl a delivery on the second day of the third Test match at The Vidarbha Cricket Association Stadium in Nagpur on 27 October 2004. India are currently 103 runs for the loss of five wickets as they chase Australia's first innings of 398 runs. (ROB ELLIOTT/AFP/GETTY IMAGES)

After just five minutes of that session I was acutely aware of the brilliant bowling mind of Shane Warne. Warne's need to bowl in the nets that day was part of his rehabilitation from a finger injury. I'd agreed to face him on the basis that it would at least provide him with a target.

Soon joining Warney at the bowling crease was WA left-arm wrist spinner Brad Hogg. Chappelli managed a few cracking cover drives off Hogg, but he was pegged down by Warne. Operating on a middle-and-leg line for 15 minutes or more, Warne bowled mainly hard-spun, dropping stock leg breaks at slightly varying paces.

After the session, Chappelli said to Warney: 'You're allowed to go up in the air around off stump you know.'

'No way,' said Warne, 'I've seen those cover drives off Hoggy.'

Chappelli realised from that exchange the sheer brilliance of Warne as a bowler.

'He (Warne) had the ability to quickly notice a batsman's strengths and weaknesses, but importantly he also had the rare skill to then land the ball where he wanted to in order to take advantage of his observations.'

Warney once confessed to Chappelli that he'd had trouble dealing with the talented West Indies batsman Carl Hooper, who was adept at using his feet to the spinners. Warney had to work him out – and he did. Chappelli asked how. Warne answered: 'I ran in to bowl with no intention of letting the ball go. As I brought my arm over I was watching his feet and that told me all I needed to know. From then on I had no more trouble with Hooper.'

Chappell always loved conversing with Warne.

All my conversations with Warney were enlightening. There was a common thread with the great spinners as I also found it fascinating to listen to Erapalli Prasanna and Muttiah Muralitharan. Warney's genius as a bowler was that he could always find a way to bemuse and confuse a batsman, he could execute any of his plans by bowling exactly where and when he wanted.

In 2000 Warne was among five players rated by *Wisden* the greatest cricketers of the 20th century. The others: Don Bradman, Garry Sobers, Jack Hobbs and Viv Richards.

For all his array of deliveries in his repertoire, much of it was Warne's bluff. He became the greatest of cricket's showmen. There were other great ones, such as Grimmett and O'Reilly, but they weren't showmen. Grimmett wheeled away, quietly weaving a web around a batsman, while O'Reilly's approach was gangling, all arms and legs, almost medium pace, attacking the right-hander's leg stump and often hitting the top of off.

Warne had lots of tricks in his repertoire, but he often just stuck to a stock leg break delivered at subtly different speeds, and a fizzing top-spinner to take out the opposition. He never forgot TJ's advice: 'Spin 'em up, Shane.' The hard-spun delivery going at the batsman in a dipping trajectory is always the hardest to combat, whether it turns in or away. As a bowler of the highest class, Warne thrived on doing the simple things brilliantly. He didn't bowl his wrong'un much and only seemed to use the zooter and the slider when his powers waned over the execution of the flipper.

Ian Healy kept to Warney for much of his career. He speaks about spin bowling in general. 'A spinner has four weapons: flight, spin, pace, angles. Field placings are another but more in the domain of the captain.' Healy continues,

The craft is to deploy combinations of the four at the right time in the match, against the appropriate batsmen. My job is to monitor the combinations being used, assess their effectiveness and maybe provide alternative options when needed. Shane Warne had absolutely the lot: skill, mental toughness, unshakeable confidence, bluff, knowledge, understanding of the opponent, accuracy and patience. His ability to be patient and continue to persist early in his career was terrific. Warney was a captain's delight.

As I have said, figures don't always tell the full story. But Warne's statistics do tell a story – and they don't lie. His record is out of this world. He took 708 Test wickets, second only to another spinner, Sri Lanka's Muttiah Muralitharan (800) and well in front of the next, another spinner, India's Anil Kumble (619). They came at an average of 25.41. He took five wickets in an innings 37 times, and 10 wickets in a match 10 times. Here are his figures in all their glory.

BATTING AND FIELDING AVERAGES

	Mat	Inns	NO	Runs	HS	Ave	BF	SR	100	50	4s	6s	Ct	St
Tests	145	199	17	3154	99	17.32	5470	57.65	0	12	353	37	125	0
ODIs	194	107	29	1018	55	13.05	1413	72.04	0	1	60	13	80	0
First-class	301	404	48	6919	107*	19.43			2	26			264	0
List A	311	200	41	1879	55	11.81			0	1			126	0
T20s	73	32	10	210	34*	9.54	228	92.10	0	0	15	7	18	0

BOWLING AVERAGES

	Mat	Inns	Balls	Runs	Wkts	BBI	BBM	Ave	Econ	SR	4w	5w	10
Tests	145	273	40705	17995	708	8/71	12/128	25.41	2.65	57.4	48	37	10
ODIs	194	191	10642	7541	293	5/33	5/33	25.73	4.25	36.3	12	1	0
First-class	301		74830	34449	1319	8/71		26.11	2.76	56.7		69	12
List A	311		16419	11642	473	6/42	6/42	24.61	4.25	34.7	20	3	0
T20s	73	71	1548	1863	70	4/21	4/21	26.61	7.22	22.1	1	0	0

Before Warne I always considered it was a toss-up between Grimmett and O'Reilly as to the best leg spinner of them all.

But having watched Warne set about working over batsmen of the ilk of Brian Lara, VVS Laxman, Sachin Tendulkar, Hansie Cronje, Kevin Pietersen and a host of others there can be no doubt in my mind. Just as those who saw Don Bradman bat in his pomp are in no doubt as to who was the greatest batsman of all, those of us fortunate enough to see Warney weave his magic are likewise in no doubt.

Shane Keith Warne was the leg spinner above all others: the greatest of his tribe.

AND ALSO

Shane Warne dominated the scene while he played, but there were others who came and went.

South Australian and Tasmanian off spinner Colin 'Funky' Miller was, like Bruce Yardley before him, a medium pacer who turned to off spin. Like Yardley he played baseball as a teenager, holding the ball between his forefinger and middle finger in the conventional manner for an off-break, but with one huge difference: he pushed down hard on his index finger with his thumb. That's how he threw an outcurve in baseball and how he bowled his off-breaks. He got the ball to really hum and was a very useful back-up bowler to Warne and co. in his time. Miller was even preferred to Warne once in the West Indies, when Warne was on the comeback trail from his shoulder injury. Miller played 18 Tests between 1998 and 2001, taking 69 wickets at the very good average of 26.15.

Once Miller turned up to a training session at the Adelaide Indoor Centre to bowl a few down to show the lads how he went about his bowling, how he trained. I asked him to say a few words to the boys and he said, 'No, mate, I can't. I know nothing about off-spin bowling. I just run in and spin it as hard as I can.'

'Well, Funky, tell 'em.'

Queensland off spinner Nathan Hauritz did some good things in his 17 Tests from 2004 to 2010, scoring 426 runs at 25.05 and taking 63 wickets at 34.98.

In 2008 off spinner Jason Krejza put his name in lights taking an incredible 12/358 against India at Nagpur. His 8/215 in the first innings included the illustrious names VVS Laxman, Rahul Dravid, Sourav Ganguly and MS Dohni. His four wickets in the next knock included the last three names on that list a second time. In Perth a month later his match figures were 1/204. And that was it. Not a spinner marked down as one for future consideration.

Victorian's Paul Jackson and Peter McIntyre were both vying for spots in the state team along with Shane Warne. Jackson, a tight and clever left-arm orthodox bowler, moved to Queensland and McIntyre, an accurate leg spinner, sought fame, if not fortune, in Adelaide. Jackson did not play Test cricket, but he excelled in first-class cricket especially after moving to Brisbane, where he was used almost exclusively to shore up an end so the fast men could attack from the other end. In 105 matches he took 240 wickets at 38.27, with three five-wicket hauls. He holds a unique record as the first player to figure in Sheffield Shield trophies for two states – Victoria and Queensland. McIntyre played 97 first-class matches, taking 322 wickets at 39.66, and two Tests, taking five wickets for 194 at 38.80.

Brad Hogg, the WA left-arm wrist spinner, played seven Test matches. He hit 186 runs at 26.57 with a highest score of 79. With the ball he struggled, taking 17 wickets at 54.88, but Hogg's main claim to spin bowling fame was his performance in one-day cricket. In 123 matches he took 156 wickets at 26.84. For much of his cricketing life Hogg was a postman in Perth – just as George Giffen was in Adelaide all those years ago. Imagine him walking the streets briskly with a saddle bag full of letters, building stamina in his legs; perfect for a spinner yearning to bowl long spells. Hoggy used to bowl with his tongue stuck out like a young, wide-eyed anteater about to pounce. Energetic to the point of hyperactivity, Hoggy was a crowd favourite. He would bat, bowl and field for any captain at any time. He had a good wrong'un and a splendid flipper, but his leg break (an off-break to a right-hander) didn't turn a great deal. Pity, because if he had operated with a slightly lower bowling arm Hoggy may have been a Test match champion.

NSW and Tasmanian off spinner Gavin Robertson played a handful of Tests for a return of 13 wickets at 39.62.

There were a few batsmen who grabbed some wickets with their spinners. Michael Clarke was one, bowling decent enough left-arm slow stuff, snaring 31 wickets at 38.19 with a career best of 6/9 against India. Two others, Darren Lehmann and Andrew Symonds could bowl a bit better than mere part-timers. Lehmann bowled left-arm slows in the orthodox way, taking 15 wickets at 27.47 in his 27 Test matches. Symonds played 26 Tests and took 24 wickets at 37.22 with his off spinners. Symonds was also a magnificent fieldsman. Mark Waugh played 128 Tests, sometimes bowling medium pace, sometimes off spin, ending with 59 wickets at 41.16. Left-arm wrist spinner Michael Bevan captured 29 wickets at 24.24.

There were many great players of spin with lightning footwork and judgement of length through the years. These greats include Victor Trumper, Don Bradman, Stan McCabe, Lindsay Hassett, Neil Harvey, Mark and Steve Waugh, Ian and Greg Chappell, Allan Border and Steve Smith. Their batting prowess helped spinners because they had to find a way to get wickets at the highest level, and the great ones invariably did so. The ongoing battle between bat and ball is all the more alluring when it is a contest between a great spinner and a master batsman.

THE WORLD
AFTER WARNE

After Shane Warne gave the game away in the wake of a sensational career that turned cricket on its head and showed how spin could be pure magic, the boffins were saying 'cricket will never be the same' and 'we will never see the like of Warne again'.

Many were tried and many fell by the wayside. South Australia's off spinner Dan Cullen looked like he might do well on the Test stage, but sadly lost his mojo at a young age. However, he had a few outstanding days with the ball for his state and played one Test match, against Bangladesh at Chattogram, alongside Shane Warne and Stuart MacGill. But Cullen was bowled sparingly, getting 1/54 for the match, while Warne and MacGill took 15 wickets between them. This was the match in which fast bowler Jason Gillespie in an extraordinary display hit an undefeated 201, having come in as a nightwatchman – in what turned out to be his last test. It was also Cullen's finale on the Test stage, the difference being that Gillespie's departure was done on his own terms. WA's left-arm orthodox bowler Ashton Agar has played four Tests yielding nine wickets, his biggest contribution being his remarkable 98 on debut at Nottingham when he batted No 11. Jon Holland, Victoria's left-arm orthodox spinner, has played four Tests taking nine wickets at 63.77; Bryce McGain, Victoria's leg spinner, played one Test against South Africa and returned figures of 0/148; Pakistani-born

Victorian-based leg spinner Fawad Ahmed has played T20 and one-day for Australia, but no Tests.

Nathan Lyon, the off spinner from SA who transferred to NSW, has become the constant way above the others.

Then there were the part-timers. WA batsman and occasional off spinner Marcus North took 14 wickets at 42.21, including an impressive 6/55 against England; Steve Smith and Michael Beer bowled tidily for a while. Smith, a leg spinner, decided to concentrate on his batting to become a world-class technician and now seldom bowls a long spell in first-class cricket; Victoria's Glenn Maxwell has bowled a few good spells in Tests, but operates best mostly in the short form of the game. Queensland leg spinner Mitch Swepson looked the goods a year or two ago, but hasn't quite kicked on, although he is young. There is still time for him. South African–born Queensland leg spinning all-rounder Marnus Labuschagne has enormous ability with bat and ball and could make a big impact down the track.

STEVE O'KEEFE

Accuracy and belief

Some spinners give the ball a big rip, others roll the ball. Steve O'Keefe is somewhere in between. He isn't a huge spinner, but he is very accurate and tends to undercut it. He mainly operates around the wicket to the right-handers and attacks the stumps relentlessly. Watching O'Keefe from the boundary you wonder how he might get a ball past a good batsman, but there is more to his bowling than meets the eye. Tight bowling is one thing; clever bowling is quite another. Steve is tight as a drum, hardly bowls a really bad ball and is clever in that he changes pace with subtle variations. In the post-Warne period many spinners were tried before the selectors turned to O'Keefe, who had for a number of seasons bagged many wickets for NSW.

Some 13 spinners were tried, most of whom faded into obscurity, leaving two main exponents of the art standing: Nathan Lyon and Steve O'Keefe. Eventually, after topping the Sheffield Shield wickets aggregate in 2014 with 41 wickets at 20.43, Steve was picked in Australia's Test squad to play Pakistan in the UAE. O'Keefe couldn't get any momentum in the Test side. He was in and out of the team for a while. Then the days of glory arrived in the first Test against India at Pune in 2017. The wicket was a big turner and O'Keefe revelled in the contest, grabbing a match haul of 12/70 – the best match figures by a visiting spinner in India. An off-field, alcohol-fuelled indiscretion soured his future with selectors in 2017, but later that year he was controversially selected for Australia's two-Test series against Bangladesh.

At the time he was suspended by NSW for his earlier indiscretion, but amazingly Cricket Australia sanctioned his recall to the Test squad. Victoria left-arm Jon Holland was preferred to O'Keefe as Australia's second spinner to Lyon for Australia's next two overseas tours, to South Africa and UAE in 2018. Holland is a bigger turner of the ball than O'Keefe and he can be economical, but he hasn't the same subtlety of changes of pace to get good players out on good wickets consistently.

O'Keefe was born in Malaysia where his father was working for the RAAF. The family returned to Australia when Steve was a toddler and he got involved in school and grade cricket. His selection in the Australian Under-19 squad in the summer of 2003–04 was a pointer of things to come for him. In 2010 he replaced the injured Nathan Hauritz in the Test squad in England, but had to cool his heels. Steve Smith was then more of a leg-spinner-cum down-the-list batsman, and he got the nod ahead of O'Keefe in the Test matches.

O'Keefe has played just nine Tests, scoring 86 runs at 9.55 with a highest score of 25. With the ball O'Keefe has taken 35 wickets at 29.40. In 83 first-class matches he has scored 2301 runs at 26.44 with a highest score of 99 and taken 285 wickets at 24.79 runs apiece. While a number of young spinners are starting to make their mark in Australia, O'Keefe may never again get the chance to grace the Test stage, but it won't be for lack of trying.

MARNUS LABUSCHAGNE

We shall see

Marnus Labuschagne is a top-order batsman who can bowl more than handy leg breaks. He scored 83 on his first-class debut with Queensland in 2014 and consistent scores, handy wickets and splendid fielding in close combined to provide him with a shock Test selection for Australia against Pakistan in 2018 on the tour of the UAE.

He is a fearless close-in fieldsman, always a boost for any side, a solid, patient batsman with an array of attacking shots, and a leggie with a good repertoire of deliveries. In his five Tests he has scored 210 runs at 26.25 and has taken nine wickets at 27.11. In 56 first-class matches he has scored 3926 runs at 37.38 with seven centuries and a high of 182. He has also taken 47 wickets at 43.89. If he can get his bowling up to speed he could become a perfect fit as a spinning all-rounder.

Labuschagne was born in South Africa, and at the age of 10 moved to Australia with his family. He grew up speaking Afrikaans, but quickly learned to speak English in his formative years.

NATHAN LYON

The groundsman who soared

There Nathan Lyon was, working as a helper to the Adelaide Oval curator one day, and the next he was picked out of the blue to play for South Australia in a Sheffield Shield match. Those sorts of fairytales always seem to happen elsewhere. There are myriad tales of young and not-so-young Pakistanis being asked to bat or bowl at the national nets in Karachi and elsewhere, only to find themselves knocking on the door of Test match selection. In Australia we had the extraordinary rise of finger-flick merchants Jack Iverson and Johnny Gleeson, both of whom came from relative obscurity in different eras, but Nathan Lyon's rise is even more of a magical carpet ride to the Test stage.

Lyon came through the junior ranks in Canberra, where he soon forged a reputation as an off spinner who really gave the ball a rip. He found work as an apprentice curator and that job brought him to Adelaide from Canberra in 2010. When resting from his oval duties, Lyon would have a bowl to the South Australia batsmen. He also bowled to the Australians in the Adelaide Oval nets and his bowling impressed Test batsman Mike Hussey, who was destined to have a big influence on Lyon's career in terms of providing help and advice and extending the hand of friendship. Lyon was spotted by Redbacks Big Bash coach Darren Berry, who had kept wicket to Shane Warne when he was playing for Victoria. Berry knew talent when he saw it and within weeks Lyon was given a try-out for South Australia's T20 squad, then he made his first-class debut. Within seven months Lyon was playing Test cricket.

On 31 August 2011 Lyon played his first Test at Galle, a picturesque harbour city in Sri Lanka. Skipper Michael Clarke said to Lyon at a drinks break: 'Ready to go?'

Lyon was fortunate to have Clarke as his first Test captain, for Clarke knows spin and spinners. Like outstanding leaders such as Ian Chappell and Mark Taylor before him, he set good, sensible and attacking fields for his bowlers. Lyon's first ball fairly buzzed from his hand; the amount of purchase he achieved had the ball dropping and curving in to left-hander Kumar Sangakkara, one of the world's best batsmen. Sangakkara came forward to defend; the ball dipped wickedly and spun, taking the outside edge, and Clarke, at first slip, dived to take a brilliant left-handed catch. After 15 overs Lyon had routed Sri Lanka; all out for 105. Lyon took 5/34 – some debut.

In the second innings he took 1/73 off 19.5 overs, and Australia won the match by 125 runs. Just four years on, Lyon had taken more Test wickets than any other Australian off spinner.

Before he was picked for the Test tour of Sri Lanka, Lyon toured Zimbabwe with Australia A. Then aged 22, the off spinner topped the wickets tally in the 50-overs format, but wasn't selected for the three-day matches. That made it all the more surprising that he was picked for Sri Lanka. After searching for a quality spin bowler in the post-Warne era, Lyon was a godsend.

There have been a few bumps along the road for Lyon. From his early days in Canberra one coach has had his eye on the off spinner.

Canadian-born John Davison was an off spinner with a classical high arm. He played first-class cricket for Canada, Victoria and South Australia, taking 111 wickets at an average of 45.61. A modest return for having twirled down in excess of 10,000 deliveries, but his figures in no way reflect his real ability. As a spin bowling coach working with all the best and emerging spinners in the land, I worked a lot with Davison.

In the nets he looked sensational. He could bowl big, top-spinning off-breaks, side-spinners and a square spinner, all deliveries that Lyon bowls today. I showed John the square spinner, the same delivery I helped Graeme Swann and Daniel Vettori with all those summers ago. In 2003 Davison stunned the West Indies by scoring the fastest century in World Cup history, but it is as a spin coach that he has made his mark, especially his relationship with Lyon.

During a Sheffield Shield match in the summer of 2013–14 I sat with two Australian selectors – Rodney Marsh and John Inverarity – at Adelaide Oval. All eyes were on Lyon. After he had bowled five balls I turned to Inverarity and said: 'He's locking his left arm. Not completing his action. Obvious problem that he must put right if he's to survive.'

Long after the Shield season had finished and in the wake of Australia's disastrous Indian campaign, I found myself at Cricket Australia's fabulous National Cricket Centre in Brisbane. I was asked by Marsh and Inverarity to run my coaching eye over Lyon. There were huge concerns about his bowling. India had won the series 4–0, but the most worrying thing for selectors was the fact that India scored heavily on big turning wickets.

There were a few spinners of potential about, including Ashton Agar and Fawad Ahmed. Selector Marsh rang often to check on the spinners' progress. Agar was steady, so too Ahmed, and both spinners were more consistent than Lyon, however instinct told me that the off spinner was far and away the best prospect of that spin trio. He was simply a small technical hitch away from being a top-flight Test bowler. To the trained eye of a good coach, Lyon was locking his lead arm and not following through properly, thus inhibiting his rhythm and putting his timing way out. A lack of consistency was all too apparent.

At training he was bowling three good balls out of 10. The other seven were dreadful. It was a great concern to all as the 2015 Ashes series in England loomed. I attempted to speak with Nathan at training. It was important that I got the message across to him. The remedy was simple: the lead arm swings back in unison with the bowling arm as it swings down past his left knee.

There was need for some repeat drills to work through to get the good feeling and comfort a bowler needs to build renewed confidence. When I approached Nathan to help, he shrugged his shoulders and refused to listen. 'No, I don't need to talk about anything. I'm okay.'

I was buoyed by his self-belief, but I wondered whether Nathan's seeming brashness was a sign of someone in denial, masking self-doubt. Over a beer that night I spoke with Greg Shipperd, then Victoria's coach. He advised me to 'write up a report and submit it at the end of the week'. Certainly, I knew Shipperd's advice was way off beam. I knew that I couldn't leave it there. That was a cop-out. If help was needed and it was required, I had to find a way. And the way forward materialised the very next day.

There was Lyon bowling away in the nets on Ray Lindwall Oval. And there was the NCC spin coach, John Davison, chatting with the young spinner. They enjoyed one another's company and I noted how Nathan listened closely to Davo's words. A voice within kept saying: 'Find a way. You must find a way, Rowdy.'

No doubt Davison was the perfect mentor for Lyon. I instinctively knew that if Lyon would not listen to me then I had to urge Davo to tell him.

Davo and I spoke for a few minutes.

'Mate, Nathan's locking his left arm. If he doesn't free his lead arm at delivery not only will he fail to take wickets and lose his Test spot, but he won't get enough batsmen out in Shield cricket to survive. He simply has to free the arm and complete his follow-through,' I said with conviction.

Within a few minutes Davo took Nathan aside. Then he showed him a replay on a video screen set up next to the net. The locking of his lead arm was obvious and Nathan must have seen it all too clearly and realised what must be done for him to return to consistency.

At that stage of his career there were grave doubts that he would go on to become anywhere near the bowler he has, for he was tentative. It was becoming difficult for a captain to set a field for him. The real turnaround in his cricket came with the realisation that he must find the sort of rhythm that would lead to consistency of length. The mindset of bowling too straight to the right-handers also had to be discarded. Nathan simply had to get outside off stump to the right-hand batsmen.

The amount of over spin he has always achieved would then give him scope to beat both edges of the bat. If it turned he had a chance to bowl a batsman 'through the gate', twixt bat and pad, and if it carried on straight as many did, often by natural variation, the outside edge came into play, thus a catch to 'keeper. The beginning of his amazing turnaround in rhythm and confidence started when he unlocked his front arm. It was the real key to his bowling.

Happily a few months later Nathan Lyon was clearing his left arm and completing his follow-through with energy. Lyon toured England in 2013, and after an early hiccup when he was overlooked in favour of Agar, he returned. He bowled so well that he was favourably compared to England's Graeme Swann, who spun well all that summer.

Nathan Lyon bowls during the first day of the second Test match between Australia and Pakistan at Sheikh Zayed stadium in Abu Dhabi on 16 October 2018. (FRANCOIS NEL/GETTY IMAGES)

Now Lyon is a top-notch Test match off spinner; by a mile the best in the world. He gets a lot of purchase on the ball and plenty of over spin. He bowls a consistent attacking line to the right-handers and makes the world's best batsmen psychologically quake in their boots. At the time of writing Lyon has taken an amazing 343 wickets at 32.54 with a best innings haul of 8/50. In 145 first-class games he has taken 510 wickets at 34.57, with 15 five-wicket hauls and two 10-wicket match hauls. No doubt he has been helped to a large degree by batsmen the world over having lost the art of footwork against the spinners. Because of the T20 wham bam bash stuff, batsmen stand and deliver. They block or slog; usually they slog. Even a top edge goes for six courtesy of big bertha bats and ridiculously shortened outfields. But in the Tests Lyon can operate with an in-out field – men up close catching and men in the deep. Batsmen the world over, even Indian players, have lost the ability to push ones and twos to break the rhythm of the bowler – and boy, does that play into Lyon's hands. At the time of writing Lyon has taken 357 wickets at 32.22 in 89 completed Tests, third on the all time list of Australian bowlers behind Shane Warne (708 at 24.41 in 145 Tests) and Glenn McGrath (563 wickets at 21.64 in 124 Tests).

At 31 Lyon is fit and keen. He is improving his batting all the time and is a brilliant fieldsman either in the outfield or close to the bat. Barring injury and loss of form, Lyon could play for a number of seasons to come and could easily exceed 500 Test wickets. Nathan Lyon, the groundsman who soared.

THE KEY TO SPIN BOWLING

Not where it lands ... how it arrives

It took me quite a while to get the gist of this thing we call spin bowling. As a youngster I toyed with off-breaks and leg breaks and could do each fairly well, although offies came more naturally to me. It wasn't until I made the trip from Perth to Adelaide to speak with the old master Clarrie Grimmett that I had any idea of how to defeat a good batsman on a true surface. I had come through the grades and succeeded to a degree. Well, I kept being promoted, probably in the hope that one day I might come good.

At the age of 16 I watched Richie Benaud bowl to Norm O'Neill at the WACA ground nets. From my position side on to the wicket I had a clear view of what was happening right in front of my eyes, yet what I saw that day was far from what was truly happening. Benaud would bowl a ball and O'Neill would block it. Then the next couple of balls, seemingly bowled at the same pace and trajectory, O'Neill would launch into a powerful off or cover drive. The pattern continued for 20 minutes or so. My conclusion: when O'Neill blocked he was resting between smashing fours. I later learned that when Benaud's trajectory was a bit flat, O'Neill drove with confidence, but when the ball was hard spun and dipping above the eye-line of the batsman O'Neill played a forward defensive shot.

But at that time I had no idea about the sensible and simple concept of getting the ball above the batsman's eye-line. So, as I said earlier, I travelled to see Grimmett and he opened my eyes to a whole new world. I came from a spinner's land of denial where my lack of wickets was due to my being a 'good bowler out of luck'. I even won selection as 12th man for a couple of Sheffield Shield games for WA, but it was not until I spoke with Grimmett that I discovered the truth.

Grimmett talked with passion about the key to spin bowling.

'It's not about where the ball lands,' he said with a grin. 'It is all about how the ball arrives.'

So spinners of all sorts need to know that if the ball arrives hard-spun, in a dipping arc, his area of danger is large, compared to a slow bowler who just rolls out the ball in a flat trajectory. Those spinners who spin hard and attain a dipping arc achieve a consistent big area to work with on the pitch; those who hardly spin it much at all need to be super accurate. Shane Warne gave the ball an almighty rip and the ball arrived humming and dipping. His area of danger was huge. Conversely Ashley Giles, the England left-arm orthodox spinner didn't spin very hard, so he needed to be accurate. His area of danger was much much smaller. Today in Australia we see the difference between Nathan Lyon and Steve O'Keefe. Lyon spins hard and dips in flight; O'Keefe, like Giles, needs to be super accurate as he doesn't get huge purchase on the ball.

Being able to attack or defend is important to any spinner.

A hard-spun stock ball, bowled at subtly different speeds, and from different points on the bowling crease, will give the spinner a real chance to take wickets consistently and, when the occasion arises, to defend successfully.

I recall NSW off spinner Gavin Robertson talking about his experience bowling to Sachin Tendulkar in India a few years back and he said, 'I'd move in and even before I let the ball go he's charge down the track and …'

'Yes, I know,' I interjected. 'Depending on his mood he's hit you for four or six.'

Gavin needed to break the rhythm of the batsman. Even a batsman of Tendulkar's class can be contained by the spinner who spins hard and operates at subtly different speeds.

It is all about spinning hard, but also changing pace in a subtle manner – because if the spinner doesn't change his pace he won't break the rhythm of the batsman. The spinner will be in for a torrid time.

Good technique is important, but every bowler is different and so long as their technique is not inhibiting what they are trying to achieve the wise coach should leave well enough alone.

It does not matter what type of spin bowler you happen to be – there is no substitute for bowling for hours at the nets. The young spinner must develop a nice easy repeatable action. It should be simple. Move in rhythmically, drive up and over the braced front leg at delivery and rotate the shoulders like a wheel. When we talk about working hard at the nets, we mean bowling as if you were bowling in a match. Work the batsman over, change pace and break the batsman's rhythm. It is important to bowl from different points of the crease so that the ball is arriving from slightly different angles. That messes with the batsman's mind – and it means he can't just keep playing the same shot.

Watch the good spinners, how they spend a lot of time on their front foot. This gives them that little bit of extra time to exert more energy on the ball and energy through the crease on follow-through. Some of Australia's best spinners of the recent past – Shane Warne, the shining example, and off spinner Tim May – spent lots of time on the front foot. Nathan Lyon has begun doing so in the past year or two and has reaped the rewards for it.

Hard work at the nets builds belief. The harder a spinner works, the more belief the spinner builds, the more success he has. This is no coincidence.

Most importantly, remember that the key to spin bowling – as Clarrie Grimmett told me in his backyard all those years ago – is not where the ball lands, but how it arrives.

APPENDIX

The Richie Benaud skincare regime

It was on my first tour of England in 1968 that Richie Benaud gave me his dilly bag with the formula for skinned spinning fingers. He discovered a cure for sore and split spinning fingers when this treatment was provided to him by a chemist in Timaru, New Zealand, in the 1950s.

The Benaud Cure
Ingredients:
1 packet of emery boards
1 packet of boracic acid powder
1 bottle of oily calamine lotion
1 packet of tissues

When a spinner loses skin off his main spinning finger, he can apply methylated spirits to harden the skinned area. However, if the skin goes too hard it will split and the problem will remain for a long time. The idea, Richie explained, was to allow the affected area to be fairly hard but flexible.

The unaffected skin next to the damaged area needs to be on much the same level, so that's where the emery board comes in. You cut away any dead skin and file to ensure there are no little bits that the seam can catch and rip. You then apply the oily calamine lotion to the affected skin and use a tissue to carefully dab off any air bubbles that appear. You sprinkle the boracic acid powder over the calamine lotion on your finger and work it into a paste. Leave for an hour and repeat.

The Benaud Cure worked nicely for me. It doesn't work for all, but I pass on Rich's formula to young spinners where I can. Maybe it will work for you.

AFTERWORD

A never-ending story

The Magic of Spin abounds in the game of cricket now as it has always done. The quality of spin has differed over the years just as the quality of the batting and fielding has. Right from the time 'Lumpy' Stevens bowled a middle stump into the game of cricket in England all those years ago, cricket has continually changed. Wickets have become truer; players' techniques in all aspects of the game have, in every succeeding generation, become better. Footwork against the spinners has declined in recent times, but hopefully that is a temporary phase in the passing parade of cricket.

Spin has always been an enchanting aspect of cricket. I have read avidly of the champions of the past: men such as CTB Turner, Clarrie Grimmett and Bill O'Reilly, being been fortunate enough to know the latter two, as well as George Tribe, Cec Pepper, then Richie Benaud, who revitalised the art. Then there was a period after Benaud in the 1980s when spin bowling, especially leg spin, was something of a lost art: gone like the dinosaurs.

Then emerged Shane Warne, who turned out to be the greatest spinner of them all. And he was a showman who always delivered, like the magician who never missed a trick and had the audience gasping in wonderment. Don Bradman never wavered from his stance that he felt Bill O'Reilly to be the best spinner he ever faced, but then he never batted against Warne. Spin bowling will always hold its own fascination, even mystery, for the generations to come. Records will be broken as they always are.

After Warne's amazing career, spin again fell away. Then came Nathan Lyon, an off spinner, who had worked as an assistant groundsman, then grabbed his chance to play first-class cricket – and boy did he grasp it with both hands. Lyon's rise to fame on the world stage was something of a magical carpet ride. But no player is above the game. Others will come. Some day others will emerge to fascinate and delight the crowds at the ground, the millions watching television and listening on the radio. This is a never-ending story: The Magic of Spin will be with us forever.

BIBLIOGRAPHY

A Century of Cricketers, AG 'Johnnie' Moyes, Angus & Robertson, Sydney and London, 1950

Benaud, Brian Matthews, Text Publishing, Melbourne, 2016

Bradman, The Illustrated Biography, Michael Page, Macmillan, South Melbourne, 1983

Great Australian Test Cricket Stories, Ashley Mallett, HarperCollins – ABC Books imprint, Melbourne, 2017

Lords Dreaming, The Story of the 1868 Aboriginal tour of England and beyond, Ashley Mallett, Souvenir Press, London, 2002

Mr Cricket, Bill Ferguson, Nicholas Kaye, London, 1950

No Spin, Shane Warne with Mark Nicholas, Penguin Random House, North Sydney, New South Wales, 2018

On Top Down Under, Ray Robinson, Cassell Australia, Stanmore NSW and North Melbourne, Victoria, 1975

Out of My Comfort Zone, Steve Waugh, Penguin Books Australia, Camberwell, Victoria, 2006

BIBLIOGRAPHY

Scarlet: Clarrie Grimmett Test Cricketer, Ashley Mallett, The Cricket Publishing Company, West Pennant Hills, Sydney, 2008

Six and Out, Jack Pollard, Pollard Publishing Company, Wollstonecraft, NSW, 1971

10 for 66 and all that, Arthur Mailey, Allen and Unwin, Crows Nest, NSW, 2008

The Summer Game, Gideon Haigh, ABC Books (revised), Sydney, NSW, 2006

The Terror, Ric Sessions, Cricket Books, Victoria, 2012

Wisden Cricketers' Almanacks 1949, 1954, 1976, Sporting Handbooks Ltd, London

Wisden Cricketers' Almanack 2001, John Wisden & Co, Hampshire

ACKNOWLEDGEMENTS

My thanks to the following people for their help in my writing this book.

Firstly my mother, Clare, who so encouraged me to bowl and bowl and bowl in the search to become the best I could be as a spinner, I cannot thank you enough. So too my brother Nick who always batted in out backyard 'Tests', which meant I had to bowl and bowl and bowl. My father, Ray, also encouraged my spin bowling and once said 'you are not flighting the ball'. He was right but he didn't know how to advise me to correct the hitch in my technique. I guess it had something to do with my going – at the age of 15 – from a little tubby kid to a tall lanky, gangling 'giraffe', having grown some 11 inches in one calendar year.

After the family moved from Sydney to Perth when I was nine years old there were some terrific influences on my cricket. AEO Barras*, an RAF pilot in WWII and a left-hand batsman and capable left-arm orthodox spinner who then played for the Mount Lawley Cricket Club and formerly with WA for a handful of matches, was

271

wonderfully encouraging. So too was Lloyd Meredith, captain of the 1958 WA State Schoolboys (now Under-17s) side, which played the Australian Championships in Adelaide. Meredith was way ahead of the pack as a young leader and, I suspect, had he developed his game to the extent of playing first-class cricket his leadership qualities would have shone.

I received fabulous support from Barry Shepherd*, the WA and Test left-hand batsman; Murray Vernon*, WA batsman; John Rutherford and Wally Langdon*, ex WA batsman and state selector, although Wally thought I was a better batsman than a bowler; Frank O'Driscoll and Trevor Bidstrup at Mount Lawley for their support and encouragement; Subiaco fast bowler and Australian baseballer Neville Pratt*, a great friend and mentor; Greg Chappell, Les Favell*, Sir Donald Bradman*, Clarrie Grimmett*, Bill O'Reilly*, George Tribe*, Neil Hawke*, Barry Jarman, Bruce Dooland* and Dennis Yagmich.

My thanks to Sandy Grant, Hardie Grant Books chief executive and director, and to ex Queensland and Test wicketkeeper John McLean for their advice.

Thanks to former WA all rounder, footballer, journalist and author Ian Brayshaw, who put me in touch with Pam Brewster, publisher at Hardie Grant Books, when I ran the concept of *The Magic of Spin* past him. Many thanks to Pam and her team, including project manager, senior editor Loran McDougall and freelance editor Michael Epis for their expertise and professionalism throughout this process of getting *The Magic of Spin* to the people. Thank you to Jim Laker and Tony Lock, two of England's and the world's finest. Also I learnt a great deal from an unlikely source during the Australian tour of England in 1968. Australia was playing Northamptonshire and I was bowling from the famous Yorkshire-born English Test umpire Syd Buller's* end. I had already taken five wickets, but, with the tailender in and seemingly going nowhere, Sid kept saying,

'Go 'round ta wicket, laad. You get 'im lbw or bowled. Go 'round, go 'round!' First ball I delivered from around the wicket hit the player's front pad. I appealed loudly and Buller immediately stood tall from his normal study in crouch, and, in the flashest of flashes, he had thrust his right index finger high. 'That's out, laad ... well bowled, well bowled!'

My thanks to Ian Chappell for writing an informative and insightful foreword. Chappelli's description of facing Shane Warne in the nets was also a gem. Thank you Ian.

My thanks to Sir Ron Brierley for his support of the Spin Australia coaching program; former Cricket Australia chairmen Jack Clarke and Creagh O'Connor; and teammates John Inverarity, Rodney Marsh and ex ABC radio host Roger Wills for their encouragement of the craft I pursue.

Inverarity was aged 13 and I was 12 when we first met in a match. Inver was playing for Scotch College and I was a member of the WA State Schoolboys Eleven. Even by that tender age Inver was being touted as a coming star bat. He likes to regale our short contest: 'His first ball was slightly short and I went back and across and hit it sweetly through point for four.' But Inver never tells what happened next. I'll give you a clue. The ball fizzed and dropped, pitching off and skipping off straight as a dye ... and Inver missed it.

Also thanks to two heroes of mine, Alan Davidson, fast bowling, hard hitting all-rounder, and Neil who was, to my mind, the best batsman Australia produced since Bradman. Both men could also turn their hand to spin. So, too, Rodney Cavalier, writer, a minister in the Wran NSW Labor Government, cricket tragic extraordinaire and life member of the SCG Trust.

My eternal thanks to Shane Warne for his agreeing to allow Hardie Grant Books to use an image of him on the cover of this book. Mark Nicholas too has been a brilliant supporter. Thank you, Mark.

ACKNOWLEDGEMENTS

Thanks to Ronald Cardwell for supplying a host of photographs; especially those hard-to-come-by images of players long past.

My wife, Patsy, deserves special mention. Patsy provided brilliant feedback on the stories that appear in the book and for other stories that I write for other publications. Patsy's insights are always invaluable and enlightening. Team Mallett is a good combination.

Ashley Mallett
Adelaide, 2019

*Deceased

ABOUT THE AUTHOR

Ashley Mallett is a former Australian cricketer who played in thirty-eight Tests and nine One Day Internationals between 1968 and 1980. Until Nathan Lyon, he was Australia's most successful off spin bowler since World War II. Ashley is a spin bowling consultant for Cricket Australia's National Cricket Centre in Brisbane and he runs an internationally recognised coaching program, Spin Australia. He has worked closely with a myriad spinners within Australia and overseas, including Sri Lanka's Rangana Herath and England's Graeme Swann. Ashley has written some thirty-three books and continues to write for newspapers and to be interviewed for his viewpoint of all matters cricket.